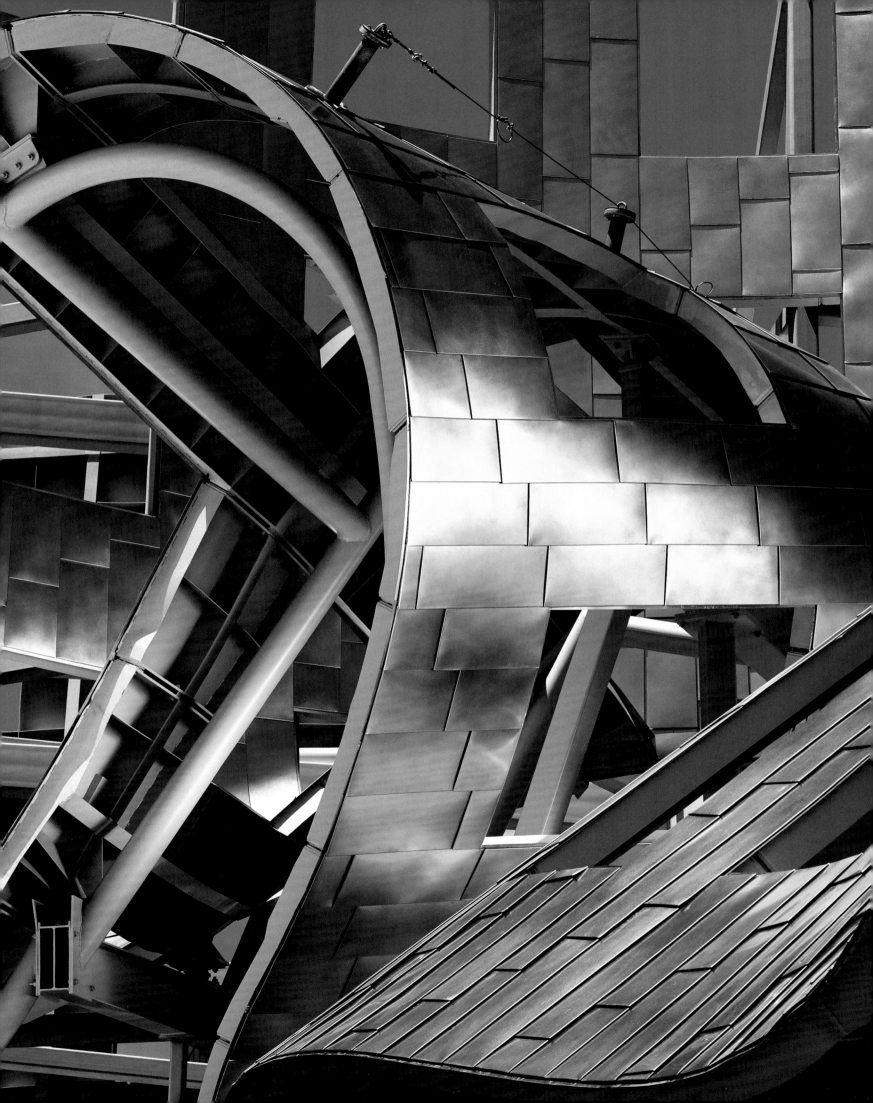

Front cover:
General view of the Luma Foundation, Arles.
Back cover:
Interior volumes of the New World Center, Miami Beach.
Pages 1–5:
Details of the Frank and Berta Gehry House,
the Marqués de Riscal Hotel,
the Lou Ruvo Center for Brain Health,
the Dr. Chau Chak Wing Building,
and the Luma Foundation.

JEAN-LOUIS COHEN

TRANSLATED FROM FRENCH
BY CHRISTIAN HUBERT

FRANK GEHRY
THE MASTERPIECES

CAHIERS D'ART | Flammarion

Frank Gehry, photographed in January 2020.

The Gehry Effect

Groundbreaking architects have always drawn sarcasm and met with incomprehension. Frank Gehry is no exception to the rule and, over the years, the seemingly arbitrary forms he has imagined have earned him many a barb, from his revolutionary house in Los Angeles to his striking museum in Bilbao. His public position against the contemporary production of architecture has hardly helped. The most shocking example was his claim that 98 percent of contemporary architecture was *sh..*, a claim that he further underscored with a raised middle finger in front of a Spanish audience in 2014. But this attitude was far from new for Gehry. It dated back to his first designs in the context of conservative and commercial Los Angeles in the 1960s.

After the ruptures introduced by the founders of modern architecture— Frank Lloyd Wright, Le Corbusier, and Mies van der Rohe—few comparable transgressions had transformed the widely accepted ways of thinking and building. The potential of industrial materials such as steel, reinforced concrete, and glass seemed to have been clearly identified, their usage established, and their aesthetic set in place. Through the explorations of Team X and the buildings of Louis Kahn and Robert Venturi, new registers of complexity, urbanity, and historicism provided alternatives to the clichés of modernity that followed once the earlier iconoclastic forms had been absorbed into mass production to the point of rendering them monotonous and sinister. It was at that moment that new and astonishing forms and spaces appeared in southern California, where the most characteristic architectural language had hitherto been that developed by Richard Neutra and his contemporaries.

The house that Frank Gehry built for his family in Santa Monica in 1978 made him a subversive in the eyes of the press. He was portrayed as having "torn up" the house—making it look like it had exploded—and having erased "the Book of Architecture" along with it.[1] This seminal building was hardly the first of his projects to have gained critical recognition. For over twenty years Gehry's creative output had already been an object of public interest. A few years previously, he had confided to a writer for a national magazine who seemed to be only just discovering him, "I want to be open-ended. There are no rules, no right or wrong. I'm confused as to what's ugly and what's pretty."[2]

This claim of ugliness served as his commentary on building elements that stood out from their neighboring bungalows through their exposed wooden frames; their prosaic, if not downright mundane, materials that were normally banned from residential construction, such as chain link and corrugated metal; and his exploration of geometric forms that were allergic to the right angle. This courage to break with accepted norms and to give new meaning to the very notion of the house was an expression of rebellion on the part of an architect trained in the orthodox modernism taught at the University of Southern California (USC) who had subsequently embarked on a search for original forms of artistic expression. It was nourished by Gehry's familiarity with the artistic circles of Los Angeles and the empathy he felt for artists working with cast-off scraps (such as Robert Rauschenberg), those staging the deconstruction of buildings (such as Gordon Matta-Clark), and minimalist sculptors (such as his close friend Larry Bell).

Gehry's fundamental reconsideration of accepted notions of the house was followed by many other revolutions, both in built and unbuilt designs. No building program that Gehry took on emerged unscathed from his interventions, whose guiding principle was to call into question forms and habits established over time. At the very moment that he was completing his scandalous house, he was creating Santa Monica Place, a shopping mall that managed the considerable feat of gaining the upper hand over the vulgarity of the boutiques within. Unfortunately, only vestiges still remain. But by

1   Sally Koris, "Renegade Gehry Has Torn Up His House—and the Book of Architecture," *People Magazine*, March 3, 1979, 78.
2   Frank Gehry, quoted by Janet Nairn, "Frank Gehry: The Search for a 'No-Rules' Architecture," *Architectural Record*, vol. 159, no. 7 (June 1976), 96.

this time he had become tired of the inevitable compromises that were part and parcel of this type of commercial project, and he turned to buildings meant for education, art, and music in order to pursue his iconoclastic project.

But even as he looked to these new fields, Gehry did not turn his back on the other main element of his professional training: the time he had spent working in Victor Gruen's office in the second half of the 1950s. In learning from the canon of gigantic shopping malls that this office had established, Gehry would adopt a working method based on the interaction of a number of specialists, from engineers to graphic designers and even acousticians and landscape designers. He discovered the importance of artificial lighting and acquired a sense for detail, but most importantly he learned to create the most striking effects with the least expensive materials. The collegiality of Gruen's office and the relationships Gehry developed there determined his way of working for years, especially through his friendship with his colleague and fellow alumnus from USC C. Gregory Walsh, who would be his associate for more than three decades.

Gehry's opportunities for creating new solutions first occurred in the sphere of music. Starting with ideas for pavilions meant for open-air concerts, he would rethink the legendary Hollywood Bowl and, over the years, propose a number of sound-diffusing devices using unusual materials: cardboard tubes or, later, plastic spheres. Working closely with the acoustician Christopher Jaffe, he built lightweight metal pavilions in Maryland and in Concord, California. These served as dry runs that would later enable him to take on more monumental programs, such as the Walt Disney Concert Hall, whose design and construction would command his attention for fifteen years. As a music enthusiast who was all the more attentive to space and sound on account of his friendship with conductors including Michael Tilson Thomas, Esa-Pekka Salonen, and Pierre Boulez, he was not content simply to settle upon some fixed principle and then repeat it. Instead, he was able to find an original configuration for every situation he encountered.

This working method, based on a sort of *tabula rasa* that rejected any limitation imposed by precedent or the expectations of the clients, would continue to guide him in one of the main domains of his creative output, the design of places for learning and research. His approach with the Loyola Law School in Los Angeles was the complete opposite of the postwar university campuses that he had frequented previously. He imagined a sort of didactic village, each part of which he developed following interminable meetings with faculty members, administrators, and students. His thoughtful attention to these discussions led him to come up with new configurations rather than recycling current ones, even though the latter might have been more reassuring. This would also hold true later, in the much more compact Stata Center at MIT, where a dialogue between offices and individual laboratories is staged in a sort of scientific citadel with an open and porous base.

None of these projects was limited to teaching and research practices as defined by bureaucratic interpretations of the program. They were based on direct interactions between the building team and the users, an indication of the importance of empathy for Gehry, without which he feels paralyzed. In retrospect, those projects he considers failures were the ones contaminated by conflicts between the projects' stakeholders. On the other hand, when friendly and even affectionate relationships were formed, they have endured over the years and led to further projects guided by reciprocal ties of loyalty. Aside from the circle of his former colleagues from the Gruen office, Gehry has maintained long-lasting friendships with individuals as diverse as the philanthropic developer James Rouse, the businessman and collector Frederick Weisman, the insurance mogul and philanthropist Peter Lewis, and the director of the Los Angeles Philharmonic, Ernest Fleischmann, as well as ties with the longtime *éminence grise* of New York architecture Philip Johnson and the art historian Irving Lavin.

As an example, an enduring loyalty would characterize Gehry's relations with Thomas Krens, the director of the Solomon R. Guggenheim Museum in New York and the force behind the creation of a worldwide network of subsidiaries. But the Bilbao branch, which contributed so much to Gehry's planetary reputation, was not his first foray into the field of art. Starting in the 1960s, with installations for the Los Angeles County Museum of Art, and with the workshops and showroom for Gemini G.E.L. in Los Angeles, he explored a number of different spatial patterns and employed prosaic materials that were destined to reappear in more permanent buildings. Running in tandem with his work with the arts, his designs for department stores such as Joseph Magnin had enabled him to master the nuances of natural and artificial lighting and to explore principles for the placement of objects in space that could be transposed from the world of merchandizing to the world of art display.

Gehry's exclusion from the competition for the design of the Los Angeles Museum of Contemporary Art in 1981 led to a deep feeling of injustice on his part, one that would subsequently be tempered somewhat by the brilliant success of his temporary installation in a nearby garage—which would ultimately become permanent. The Temporary Contemporary benefited from a loose spatial definition, but not a neutral one, and this soon became a tool that could be adapted to the most diverse installations, as Gehry himself demonstrated in 1983 with Lucinda Childs's ballet *Available Light*, whose stage set consisted of platforms and partitions formed out of steel mesh. Since his provisional California Kunsthalle was contained within a pre-existing building envelope, it barely allowed Gehry to explore the sculptural potential of the museum program, as he was beginning to do at the time in the Aerospace Museum, fragmented into volumes that inserted a sort of geometrical fanfare into a rather banal context.

Working on the other side of the Atlantic for the first time, Gehry took the modest program for the Vitra museum in Weil am Rhein as an occasion to make a significant new transition in his architectural language, by emphasizing the spiral stairs on the exterior, arranged around galleries bathed in soft, natural light. In this building, the centripetal layout of the Aerospace Museum, where the institution clustered around the galleries, was now inverted. The development of Gehry's larger projects, as well as his houses from 1978, would henceforth consist of fragmenting different program elements—galleries, auditoria, offices, and circulation spaces—whose final arrangement would be settled on only after a sometimes considerable number of variants had been studied both in model form and in Gehry's conceptual sketches.

While the white walls and zinc roofs of Vitra fit comfortably into the architectural landscapes of southern Germany and nearby Switzerland, the museums that Gehry proposed in the next decade, such as the Weisman Museum and the Bilbao Guggenheim, were clad in metallic outer skins, in screens of brick, as in the MARTa, or in a *mille-feuille* of concrete and glass, in the case of the Louis Vuitton Foundation. Their freedom of composition is not simply the result of an agglomeration of program elements. It is made possible by steel structures that are generally invisible or barely revealed. In this respect, Gehry had freed himself from the rationalist method inspired by the theories of the nineteenth century that had dominated modern architecture up until that time. He had achieved this freedom through the pragmatic systems of Gruen's commercial buildings, then over the course of his projects in southern California, with the lightweight wooden construction typical of the American West, known as the "balloon frame," so called because of its light weight and its ability to span vast spaces, whose potential he fully exploited before applying its strategies to other materials.

This structural pragmatism, or, rather, this indifference to the effects generated by structure, ended up being called into question in some of his more recent projects. In the realm of museums, the Biomuseo of Panama City, open to the sea breezes, makes no mystery of its metal structure, all the more so because it suggests analogies to the forests stretching from the Tropics to the Equator. The reinforced-concrete framing elements of the Dr. Chau Chak Wing Building and the Luma Foundation are clearly visible as they cross the interior spaces in diagonals. But even in these cases, the building forms are not mechanically determined by the constraints of the structure. Gehry's involvement in new technologies is focused on other interests. He is more invested in innovative uses of materials like glass, molded into curved or twisted forms, and in perfecting thin metal facings. In both cases, prototype fragments of a future building are mocked up at full scale, in close collaboration with providers, fabricators, and building contractors.

It is precisely this determination to master building technologies completely, from the earliest designs to the cost estimates, that led Gehry, despite his initial misgivings, to become an undisputed pioneer of digital architecture: he realized he could maintain and even extend his personal touch in the projects despite his reluctance to use the computer. Toward the end of the 1980s, he was one of the first professionals to use digital devices not only for management, structural calculations, and the background of perspective renderings, but also to define complex curves that could be calculated and evaluated without incurring astronomical estimates from contractors out of fear of the unknown. The digitization of models made it possible to explore their every dimension and to rework them easily, as was the case in the lengthy development of the house for Peter Lewis in Lyndhurst, Ohio, which ultimately remained unfinished. The Bilbao museum would provide the first window onto this new form of practice. For the aeronautics buff that Gehry had been in his youth, it is ironic that his choice of computer program would be CATIA, developed by Dassault to design and produce warplanes.

The Playa Vista office rapidly became a laboratory for computer-aided conceptual design and fabrication, to the point of creating what in the end has been a very profitable ad-hoc spinoff, Gehry Technologies. This metamorphosis came as a profound surprise, insofar as Gehry had previously been considered a technophobe artist, almost lost among the architects. It is true that his relationship with art and artists, as it has developed over time, is as intense as it is complex. Initially it formed around his daily proximity to and friendship with creative artists in Los Angeles and New York, whose work he collected, and through the exhibitions he curated at LACMA. Some artists also became his clients. This led to a number of happy results, such as the house and studio for Ron Davis and projects for Chuck Arnoldi, and sometimes ended in frustration, as with the unbuilt house for Ed Ruscha.

Gehry's interactions with Claes Oldenburg and Coosje van Bruggen, who drafted him as an actor for *Il Corso del Coltello*, a show staged at the Venice Biennale in 1985, were more complex in nature. He obtained the commission for the Vitra Design Museum through them, and they collaborated with him on the Chiat/Day building in Venice, California, for which they recycled a pair of binoculars that had previously been proposed for an uncompleted project for Venice, Italy. A proposal submitted by Gehry and Richard Serra for a 1981 competition in New York for paired teams of architects and artists remains another important moment in this story, if for no other reason than that it launched the architect on his exploration of fish and their scales.

Beyond the commissions from, the company of, and his collaborations with artists, the imprint of art is incised into the very nature of Gehry's work.

Gehry has in fact continuously sought to integrate painterly or sculptural effects into his projects. In Giorgio Morandi's still lifes he found ways of assembling objects that he employed in the Lewis House and the Experience Music Project in Seattle. The empty *piazze* of Giorgio de Chirico provided the source—in the manner of the "plagiarism by anticipation" set out by the critic Pierre Bayard[3]—for the common spaces of the Loyola Law School. In looking at sculptors, he had the revelation that the stone hoods of Claus Sluter's *Mourners* in Dijon presaged the sinuous contours and the play of shadows in the "horse's head" he inserted into the DZ Bank in Berlin, and that the draped folds of *Saint Teresa in Ecstasy*, as sculpted by Gianlorenzo Bernini, prefigured those of 8 Spruce Street in New York.

In addition to that of an artist who has lost his way, another dismissive image of Gehry has also come to the fore: that of an architect who conceives of buildings as bachelor machines, indifferent, if not downright hostile, to their context. It is true that Gehry has taken some pleasure in introducing dissonance into the cities where his projects have been built, and that he has rejected all mimetic qualities in his buildings, all literal reproduction of existing materials and design. But at the same time he has been careful to respect the specific features of their sites, to adjust their points of access, and to identify potential moments for monumental accents that could enhance the fluidity and diversity of the urban landscape. No building has been designed without the construction of at least one large model that would convey the visual impact of the construction from many blocks away. Often, several models at different scales, some of them seeming exceedingly oversized, can be found around the office, enabling the slow ripening of the project through everyday observation, yielding an inventive solution in the end.

Gehry intended to study urban design as part of his professional training but ended up registering for a planning program that did not deal with the shape of cities. His sensitivity and capacity for conceiving urban space derive more from his experiences in Victor Gruen's firm. Between 1960 and 1980, he worked on a number of urban studies for Los Angeles and several other American cities but succeeded in completing only two residential projects in Orange County, both of which remain perfectly intact today. His most ambitious project, for downtown Santa Monica, was blocked by powerful neighborhood associations and was ultimately limited to the Santa Monica Place shopping mall, which was very subtly linked to the street grid around it, unlike many comparable programs. While Gehry was talented at putting together picturesque ensembles, such as the Loyola Law School or the Edgemar Development, he was also committed to establishing just the right place for the insertion of his buildings, their relevant orientation, and ultimately the most readable configuration of their superstructures in the urban landscape. His buildings assumed responsibility for creating a focus where there was none and sharing their aura with their neighbors as a result.

But how does one accurately define Gehry's architectural position, informed as it is by the three fields of art, technique, and urban space? He has had many a label applied to him, ever since his work became known beyond the limits of Los Angeles, but none has ever managed to portray his approach perfectly. He participated in two of the most public displays of his generation, and yet he was out of synch in both of them. In 1980, Gehry's own installation for the Strada Novissima—created for the Venice Biennale by Paolo Portoghesi, and which remains to this day the first manifestation of architectural postmodernism—eschewed the historicist games that his neighbors indulged in, and addressed in the simplest manner possible the space of the Corderie dell'Arsenale. Eight years later, he was one of

3   Pierre Bayard, *Le Plagiat par anticipation* (Paris: Éditions de Minuit, 2009).

the seven architects enrolled under the banner of "deconstructivism" in a memorable exhibition at the Museum of Modern Art in New York, but only the resemblance between the wood framing projecting from his 1978 model for the Familian House and a 1920s stage set by Lyubov Popova could justify his inclusion.

Characterized in turn as an anarchist, pop artist, postmodernist, and deconstructivist, criticized for the "narcissism" of his buildings, Gehry has followed his own path, sometimes absorbing the themes of the moment from the sidelines, but more often drawing on his previous work for inspiration in a self-referential manner. The arrangement of models on the tables and shelves of the Playa Vista studio crystallizes his principle of keeping a large portion of previous work visible on a daily basis to the designers who are looking to enlarge on it. A double form of migration is made possible: new buildings are designed in the presence of their predecessors, and specific forms are removed from one model and added to another, irrespective of their initial program or scale. To give just one example, the volume at the center of the DZ Bank, which is in the shape of a horse's head, was inserted *in extremis* into the model during the competition charrette stage, and itself derived from one that appeared in several versions of the Lewis House.

Despite the fecundity of this repertoire of several hundred projects, with their different stages preserved in models, photographs, and the sketches that Gehry continued to produce even as the office entered the digital age, original and innovative forms have never ceased to appear on the screens and worktables. Opposed to the complacent facility of so many aging architects, Gehry has been able to hold onto a form of uncertainty, even a candor, that encourages him to begin each project as if with a blank slate and to hesitate before putting an end to any design.[4] Marked in some cases by hundreds of study models in wood or cardboard, these explorations are undertaken together with the office team in open conversations that are sometimes difficult to cut short in favor of action. Rather than being "patient," as Le Corbusier claimed his creative search to be, Gehry's has remained anxious and animated.

The present book joins a collection of publications devoted to Gehry's production since the 1980s, but it will neither replace those that provide an account of each of his projects, built or not, nor take the place of monographs on single buildings or the volumes of the catalogue raisonné of his drawings, which began publication in 2020.[5] It is intended to put forward an overall view of his built work and limits itself to major milestones—a little fewer than forty buildings selected from among the roughly 180 erected throughout the world over the course of six decades.

It may seem paradoxical to apply the label of "masterpiece," with all its academic and celebratory connotations, to the projects featured here, especially if one considers Gehry's deliberate decision to position himself outside of institutional and professional networks from the outset. But a return to the origins of the term enables us to consider its original meaning. When we open *The Book of Trades*, compiled by Étienne Boileau, the provost of Paris, at the end of the thirteenth century, we reads that a "masterpiece" is none other than an "crucial work," a piece that qualifies an apprentice to be considered a master of his craft.[6] If we keep this definition in mind, then the buildings documented in these pages should not simply be considered as shining examples of Gehry's inventiveness, even if they unquestionably are that. Instead, they should be understood as his restless attempts to be recognized as a different kind of architect, freed from the clichés and codes of a fundamentally conservative profession whose comfortable practice he has rejected.

4   On the phenomenon of aging, see Edward Said, *On Late Style: Music and Literature against the Grain* (New York: Pantheon, 2006).

5   Jean-Louis Cohen (ed.), *Frank Gehry, Catalogue Raisonné of the Drawings: Volume One, 1954–1978* (Paris: Cahiers d'Art, 2020).

6   See *Règlement sur les arts et métiers de Paris rédigé au XIIIᵉ siècle et connu sous le nom du Livre des métiers d'Étienne Boileau* (Paris: G.-B. Depping, 1837), 216.

The Masterpieces

Oblique view from Highland Avenue.

Hillcrest Apartment Building

Santa Monica, 1961–62

The façade on Highland Avenue.

The courtyard and the external staircases.

When it was finished, people thought
we had remodeled an old house.

Frank Gehry, quoted in Peter Arnell et al., *Frank Gehry: Buildings and Projects* (New York: Rizzoli, 1985), 20.

Economic determinants in the local, very competitive
apartment market seem to preclude the creation of
livable apartments and this building was used to explore
the realities and myths of this premise. Each apartment
enjoys a view, has a fireplace, is sound insulated from
the other apartments and has a private outdoor space....
The building is designed to harmonize with the traditional
architectural forms in the neighborhood.

"Descriptive Data, 1963 AIA Honors Award Program," 2. Gehry Partners.

Hillcrest Apartment Building

2807 Highland Avenue, Santa Monica, 1961–62

After completing the Steeves House in Bel Air in 1959, and upon his return from a year spent in Paris, Frank Gehry and his associate C. Gregory Walsh built a small apartment building on a sloping site in the Ocean Park area of southern Santa Monica. This neighborhood of bungalows built at the beginning of the twentieth century was then in full transformation. The smaller wood structures were being replaced, one after another, by bulky and featureless rental apartment buildings, known locally as "dingbats." The Hillcrest project was funded by the developer Wesley Bilson, with financial support from Gehry's mother and father-in-law, and with the input of several engineers.

The six apartments sit atop a half-buried garage and are laid out symmetrically on two floors, with access via a footpath leading to an open planted courtyard, and open-air staircases leading up from there. The structure stands on an exposed concrete-block foundation wall, in the manner of European neo-brutalist edifices, and the rendered exterior walls employ the wood framing typical of the American West. The solution adopted for the roof distinguishes it from the other apartment buildings that had pushed up like mushrooms in the area. On two sides the flat roof is concealed behind sloping planes clad in wood shakes and pierced by the chimneys that give the building its distinctive silhouette.

The relation between the angled roof and the side wall below is articulated by a chevron that is both geometrical and boldly colored, its gray wood contrasting with the white coating of the wall. It recalls certain shapes from the motels implanted along the Los Angeles boulevards during the 1950s. The reassuring vocabulary of the roofs and wooden balconies functions as a kind of camouflage netting around the orthogonal volume, from which only the kitchens cantilever out slightly. According to Gehry's recollections, the stratagem used for the roof displeased the architecture critic Esther McCoy, of whom Gehry was very fond, and who at the time was engaged in the rediscovery of the first modern Los Angeles architects, starting with Rudolf Schindler. She did not recognize the playful irony of the project— one that the mayor of Santa Monica, Thomas M. McCarthy, considered "an outstanding example of what our free enterprise system can achieve in this area of activity when the building of our neighborhoods is in the hands of enlightened private developers and architects who will accept the challenge of modern buildings."[1]

The arrangement of the interiors expresses the enthusiastic manner in which Gehry and Walsh were looking to Japan at the time. They borrowed several traditional Japanese elements and inserted them into the apartments' ingenious layouts. Sliding doors divide the bedroom from the living room, and a clerestory wood beam, inspired by Japanese openwork *ranma*, marks the passage between the dining and living rooms. Over the years, the inhabitants of this first refined residence by Gehry would include the architect himself, his psychoanalyst, Milton Wexler, and the artist Judy Chicago, among others.

Interior views of the living and dining rooms of an apartment.

The entrance of the residence on Melrose Avenue.

Lou Danziger Studio and Residence

Los Angeles, 1964–65

The Danziger Studio had to be plaster. And I wanted a raw, rough texture. I was looking at [Louis] Kahn a lot, but I was also looking at [Le] Corb[usier]. Whatever was in my consciousness, I loved rough stucco. No buildings were done with that. They call it "tunnel mix." It was underneath the freeways.

Frank Gehry, quoted in Mildred Friedman (ed.), *Gehry Talks: Architecture + Process* (New York: Rizzoli, 1999), 46–47.

The corner of the residence on Melrose Avenue.

Lou Danziger Studio and Residence

7001 Melrose Avenue and Sycamore Avenue, Los Angeles, 1964–65

In his legendary 1971 book *Los Angeles: The Architecture of Four Ecologies*, Reyner Banham ignored practically all contemporary production but still made sure to include the cubic building that Gehry had built on Melrose Avenue. This project was no doubt the first to be noticed by Gehry's colleagues and by artists in Los Angeles because of its geometry and rough surfaces. The graphic designer Lou Danziger, who worked frequently with the Los Angeles County Museum of Art, intended to set up both his studio and his residence in this neighborhood, where many printers were based.

The first sketches drawn by Gehry and Walsh included both program elements in a single volume, which they soon redivided into two parts. Traffic noise led them to conceive of opaque boxes closed off from the avenue, with only a single kitchen window facing it. As the architects put it, "The dirty, noisy and totally public nature of the surroundings necessitated completely introverting and screening the building from the street. The solution was a fortress-like structure, recessed from the street, with the residential part sequestered behind a high wall."[1]

Inside the studio, where a darkroom forms a box within the box, the walls are finished in plaster while the wood ceiling structure, the electrical conduits, and the ventilation system are all left exposed—as in the SoHo lofts that Gehry had recently begun to frequent on his many trips to New York. He also decided to avoid the uniform lighting conditions that were typical of this sort of program and that would have resulted from using only north-facing skylights: "I mixed the light at the back end and through the skylight, so it was not obtrusive, but it was mixed above eye level."[2]

The urban landscape of Los Angeles became a more complex source of inspiration than in the Hillcrest apartments and the projects that followed it. The concrete texture banally used for tunnels was employed as a finish on the same wooden structures as in the "dumb boxes," those monotonous buildings lining the city thoroughfares that Gehry had emulated the year before, in the nearby offices and workshop designed for Faith Plating. The articulation of the volumes on the exterior recalls Irving Gill's Horatio Court West, built in Santa Monica in 1915, which Esther McCoy had exhumed five years before in her *Five California Architects*. Reyner Banham also remarked that "What is important and striking is the way in which this elegantly simple envelope not only reaffirms the continuing validity of the stucco box as Angeleno architecture, but does so in a manner that can stand up to international scrutiny. The cycle initiated by Schindler comes round again with deft authority."[3] It certainly caught the eye of David Hockney, who was living in Los Angeles at the time. His *Picture of Melrose Avenue in an Ornate Gold Frame* of 1965 includes a solid gray rectangle that is difficult not to associate with the Danziger cubes.

1   "Descriptive Data, 1970 AIA Honors Award Program." Getty Research Institute.
2   Quoted in Rosemarie Haag Bletter (ed.), *The Architecture of Frank Gehry* (New York: Rizzoli, 1986), 185.
3   Reyner Banham, *Los Angeles: The Architecture of Four Ecologies* (Harmondsworth: Penguin Books, 1971), 198.

General view from Sycamore Avenue.

Frontal view from Melrose Avenue.

The entrance to the studio on Melrose Avenue.

The studio interior, with the cube-shaped darkroom at left.

Lou Danziger playing pool in the studio.

Ed Moses (left), Frank Gehry (center), and Ron Davis (right) in front of the house.

Ron Davis Studio and Residence

Malibu, 1968–72

View of the site and the surrounding landscape.

View of the house with the Pacific in the distance.

I was nervous about that project; I thought the degree of the angles might be bizarre, and make you feel uneasy. In fact, it was very restful. The building unlocked a whole lot of other possibilities for me. I spent a lot of time there, sitting and looking for a lot of days and evenings, watching the reflections.... Because nothing was parallel, you couldn't predict where the shadows and sunlight and reflections would fall. If you've got a straight rectangular box, with rectangular windows, you sense where these things come from. But if things aren't all straight then you get a different take.

Frank Gehry, quoted in Peter Arnell et al., *Frank Gehry: Buildings and Projects* (New York: Rizzoli, 1985), 58.

Ron Davis Studio and Residence
29715 Cuthbert Road, Malibu, 1968–72
Destroyed in the 2018 Woolsey Fire

In 1976, the *Architectural Record* published the first article on Gehry's building designs to appear in a national magazine. Up until that point, Gehry had been known primarily for his cardboard furniture, whose commercial success had been short-lived. But here was a clear statement of his position in relation to art: "I search out the work of artists, and use art as a means of inspiration. I try to rid myself, and the other members of the firm, of the burden of culture and look for new ways to approach the work."[1]

The Malibu house illustrates this attitude, as well as Gehry's perplexity regarding "what's ugly and what's pretty." It is directly linked to the issues raised by the work of the young painter Ron Davis, whose geometric deformations inspired its shape, and it employs corrugated metal, that "ugly" material that Gehry had previously used in 1968 for a Billy Al Bengston exhibition at LACMA, and for the Donna O'Neil barn in San Juan Capistrano.

The façades' visual distortions were the result of experiments that Gehry and Davis conducted in the field, where they often met to stretch out strings and establish vanishing lines for the perspectives they sought to create. According to Gehry, "The shift from orthogonal to perspectival came from Ron Davis because he was doing paintings that were about perspectival constructions. I was fascinated by the fact that he could draw but he could not make them; he could not turn them into three-dimensional objects.... I put vanishing points on the wall with a pen and then I took strings and pinned them down to the site model, in the center of the room."[2]

As for Gregory Walsh, he recalled that "originally it started out to be a rather complicated exercise, taking a perspective image that was drawn with the vanishing points, and then having another perspective rising out of the original perspective."[3] When the almighty architect and patron Philip Johnson came from New York, he was puzzled by the configuration and said, "It looks like there are vanishing points, but where are they?"[4] After that visit, Johnson would become an active supporter of Gehry's work.

Wooden frames in Douglas fir provided the freedom not only to create the overall form, but also to open up a variety of windows within it. The roofing structure was left exposed on the inside, reiterating the approach Gehry had taken in the Danziger studio and creating a wooden sky with plastered partitions below. It was as if a New York feel had been transposed to the Pacific coast and combined with that of a Mediterranean village. According to Davis, Gehry "proposed putting everything on wheels, including the wall partitions and stairs, so that I could continually alter the shape and mix of the rooms."[5] But this potential flexibility was never utilized.

1   Quoted in Janet Nairn, "Frank Gehry: The Search for a 'No-Rules' Architecture," *Architectural Record*, vol. 159, no. 7 (June 1976), 95.
2   Quoted in Alejandro Zaera-Polo, "Conversations with Frank O. Gehry," in *Frank Gehry 1987–2003* (Madrid: El Croquis, 2006), 25.
3   Quoted in Mildred Friedman, *Frank Gehry: The Houses* (New York: Rizzoli, 2009), 127.
4   Quoted in Paul Goldberger, *Building Art: The Life and Work of Frank Gehry* (New York: Alfred A. Knopf, 2015), 169.
5   Marshall Berges, "Ron Davis: He Plays Tricks with Dimensions," *Los Angeles Times Home*, August 17, 1975, 10.

The studio mezzanine.

The mezzanine and the bridge connecting the studio with the living quarters.

The studio featuring two paintings by Frank Stella (right).

View of the inner courtyard.

Offices and workshops of Gemini G.E.L.

Los Angeles, 1976–79

General view from Melrose Avenue.

Oblique view of the first building, on Melrose Avenue.

Most frame buildings look great under construction, but when they're covered they look like hell. So I was trying to capitalize on that, and see if there wasn't a way to capture the good side of the equation.

Frank Gehry, quoted in Rosemarie Haag Bletter (ed.), *The Architecture of Frank Gehry* (New York: Rizzoli, 1986), 56.

The wood frame of the second building under construction.

Offices and workshops of Gemini G.E.L.
8365 Melrose Avenue, Los Angeles, 1976–79

Despite the apparent banality of the volumes lining the street, the buildings designed for Gemini G.E.L. (Graphic Editions Limited), which included both renovation and new construction, mark an important moment in the step-by-step process by which Gehry distanced himself from the rigidity of traditional practice. In this double intervention, located a few blocks away from the Danziger studio, he continued to work with the local vernacular construction of Los Angeles but broke with its repetitive character in order to achieve a new freedom.

In 1966, Sidney B. Felsen, Stanley and Elyse Grinstein, and Kenneth Tyler invested in a warehouse built some twenty years earlier with the intention of producing multiples of works by New York artists such as Robert Rauschenberg, Richard Serra, and Elsworth Kelly, as well as artists from Los Angeles including Ed Ruscha and Edward Kienholz. Gehry would subsequently transform this initial foothold in two distinct phases of work.

The first intervention consisted of enclosing the existing volume in a new wooden façade, finished off with a green coating, that reframes but still reveals the original doors and their surrounds, all the while affording a view of the activities taking place inside. An oblique rooftop element extends this sloping volume, which appears to be attached to a suspended advertising billboard, as if illustrating Robert Venturi's notion of "inflection," used to describe the implied connection between Baroque churches in Rome and their immediate surroundings.[1]

A more ambitious program was subsequently undertaken, along the same lines as the first but reflecting the growing success of Gemini. It included "a silk screen and etching workshop, an artist's studio, availability gallery (featuring specially designed display carousels) and a documentation room."[2] These spaces are housed in an L-shaped building finished off with white stucco on the exterior. It is located to the west of the first one, with two narrow courts separating the buildings. The joint between them is neither concealed nor camouflaged, but instead becomes the project's main theme.

On the inside, the wood frame allows for a play of forms that makes the Ron Davis studio seem timid in comparison. The struts of the upper level seem to attack the white box in two ways. Part of the flooring on the upper level is amputated in order to bring light down to the ground floor, even as it collides with the main volume. The lower volume of the first building remains a stable form, but the structures of the hallway and stairs inside seem to be in revolt against it. The visually arresting frame gives a dramatic character to two buildings that might otherwise have formed a perfectly peaceful couple. The screen of wood studs is no longer subservient to an architecture of smooth volumes but exposes itself to the street instead.

In its finished state, the façade on Melrose Avenue partly reveals the mysteries of the interior it shelters, in which the relations that Gehry established with artists, critics, and art dealers on both American coasts are reflected.

1   Robert Venturi, *Complexity and Contradiction in Architecture* (New York: Museum of Modern Art, 1966), 91–97.
2   Office description, 1979. Gehry Partners.

The juncture between the two buildings, as seen from Melrose Avenue.

The exposed wooden structure.

The interior staircase.

One of the workshops.

The window at the corner of 22nd Street and Washington Avenue.

Frank and Berta Gehry House

Santa Monica, 1977–78

View from 22nd Street, with the original bungalow visible behind the corrugated metal wall.

The glass prism overlooking Washington Avenue.

My wife, Berta, found this beautiful anonymous little house, and I decided to remodel it, and since it was my own building, explore ideas I'd had about the materials I used here: corrugated metal and plywood, chain link. I was interested in making the old house appear intact inside the new house, so that from the outside, you would be aware always that the old house was still there. You could feel like this old house was still there and some guy just wrapped it in new materials, and you could see, as you looked through the windows—during the day or at night—you would see this old house sitting in there.

Frank Gehry, quoted in Rosemarie Haag Bletter (ed.), *The Architecture of Frank Gehry* (New York: Rizzoli, 1986), 32.

Frank and Berta Gehry House
22nd Street and Washington Avenue, Santa Monica, 1977–78

At the corner of two streets on a peaceful residential block, this house scandalized the neighbors and marked a turning point both for Gehry and for world architecture. By carving up an existing house and embracing it, as it were, in an extension that occupied the setback separating the house from its boundary, he transformed the conventional arrangement of domestic space. The initial incisions into the house cannot help but recall his familiarity with Gordon Matta-Clark's series of interventions known as *Splitting*. Gehry's use of materials typically overlooked in residential construction, such as chain link, corrugated metal, or raw plywood, were in the same vein as the ready-mades created by Marcel Duchamp, whose work he had seen in the first one-man exhibition devoted to the artist at the Pasadena Art Museum in 1963. In a lecture of 1976, Gehry theorized the use of "poor" and prosaic materials as "cheapskate architecture,"[1] thus making a virtue out of necessity in view of the limited resources he had at his disposal. Gehry conceived this house as fluid and continuous, in which space appropriated from an access path would become a linear kitchen, lined with a cabinet built into the window of the original bungalow. The interior partitions were finished in raw plywood or stripped down to expose their internal structure, which provided warmth to the living room and upstairs bedrooms. This continuum of wood highlights those elements that have been preserved—the windows now transformed into frames, for instance, along with the moldings and the cornices.

The imagination at work in the house's spatial organization is redoubled in the design of the openings. One of them, cut out of the perimeter wall, provides a view of a cactus and a brace to passers-by, as if exposing the back side of a Hollywood set. Other openings set into the same wall are glass volumes rather than simple surfaces. The most spectacular of them is a glazed prismatic block that appears to belong to neither the original house nor the extension, and that seems ready to pop out of the wall and fall on the sidewalk.

There is no overriding obsession with unity in this collage of heterogeneous pieces. On this subject, Gehry would say that, "instead of a house being one thing, it's ten things, it allows the client more involvement, because you can say, 'Well, I've got ten images now that are going to compose your house. Those images can relate to all kinds of symbolic things, ideas that you have liked, places you've liked, bits and pieces of your life that you would like to recall.'"[2] This provocative project was immediately praised by critics and earned Gehry international fame, leading to his invitation to the Venice Architecture Biennale of 1980. In an editorial in *Domus*, Alessandro Mendini saw it as "a heap of pieces all on top of and inside each other," in which "the magma that holds these 'cultural' parts together is conversely a pile of urban leftovers, fragments of fences, scaffoldings, sheds, rolling shutters and electric light poles. The whole thing is 'fixed' not in the final phase, but on the building site or during dismantling, with wires, piping, windows, walls and floors 'locked' in their place."[3] Between 1991 and 1994, Gehry would adapt it to his children's needs. He would cover parts in sheet metal and create somewhat more polite additions, as if he regretted having been so provocative to his neighbors.

1   Frank Gehry, "Cheapskate Architecture," lecture at Rice University, Houston, November 1, 1976.
2   Quoted in Rosemarie Haag Bletter (ed.), *The Architecture of Frank Gehry* (New York: Rizzoli, 1986), 47.
3   Alessandro Mendini, "Dear Frank Gehry," *Domus*, no. 604 (March 1980), 1.

The living room, featuring the original fireplace.

The dining area, with a window giving onto Washington Avenue.

The kitchen and one of the windows retained from the original bungalow (left).

View of the living room and the wood frame of the original bungalow.

The chain-link superstructure on Washington Avenue.

The dining area, featuring a work by Chuck Arnoldi.

The Fritz B. Burns building, with its exterior stairs.

Loyola Law School

Los Angeles, 1978–2003

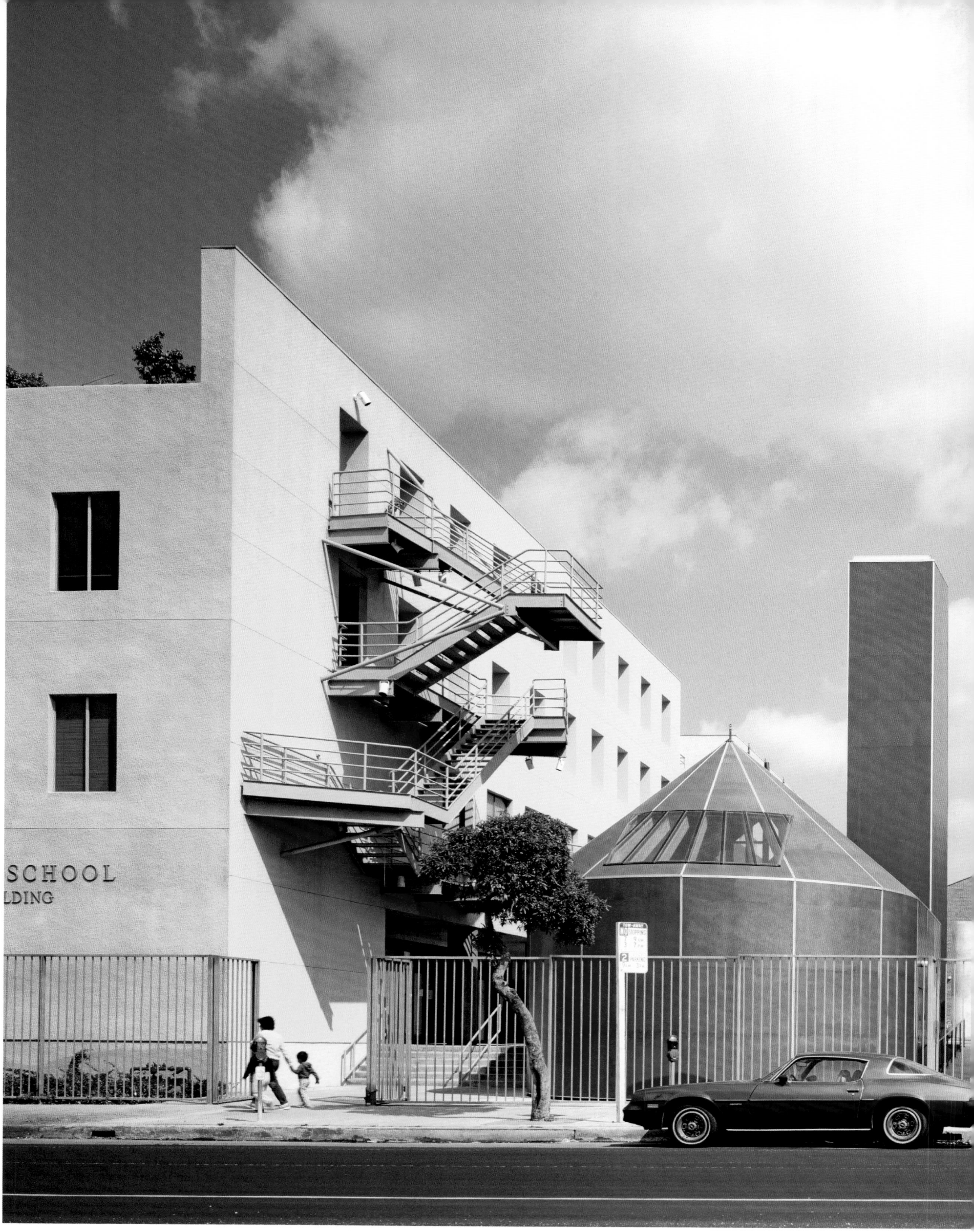
SCHOOL

The campus as seen from Olympic Boulevard.

The main stairs of the Fritz B. Burns building.

Bird's-eye view of the campus from the northeast.

I was concerned about making a place for the study of law. And we continued to work with this client.... It all related to the clients and the students saying, from the very first meeting, saying they felt denied a place, a sense of place. So, the whole idea here was to create that kind of space in downtown in a neighborhood that was difficult to fit into it. And, it was my theory, or my point of view that one didn't upstage the neighborhood, one accommodated. I've tried to be inclusive, to include the buildings in the neighborhood whether they were buildings I liked or not.

Frank Gehry, "Defending a Vision for Architecture," lecture, TED Talks, 1990.

Loyola Law School
919 S. Albany Street, Los Angeles, 1978–2003

In 1978, the faculty and administration of the Jesuit Loyola Law School decided to expand its campus situated to the west of central Los Angeles. They drew up a list of potential architects, with a clear preference for Charles W. Moore. Yet Gehry obtained the commission during the course of an interview in which he persuasively shared his understanding of the pedagogical and institutional issues involved. His notebook from meetings with the clients conveys his readings of their expectations. He jots down notes about the "traditionalism of [the] legal profession," indicates that the "faculty [is] divided on importance of library: research oriented vs. practice oriented," and underscores the "dehumanization" of the students, who "learn more from fellow students than from professors from law school."[1] His relationship with Robert Benson, the professor most engaged in the project, would become so close that he would build Benson's house in Calabasas.

There were seven successive phases of building along Olympic Boulevard before the campus was complete. The first two phases—which conformed closely to the overall plan—were the most remarkable, because in certain ways they constitute an urban counterpart to the manifesto that Gehry had created in the form of his house. Unlike the fabric of that neighborhood, which Gehry knew well, having lived there in his youth, the new campus needed to be considered as an organic entity, not as an assemblage of independent buildings, so as to conform to the school's teaching philosophy in the closest possible way.

For Gehry, who had been interested in urban composition ever since his formative years, this project was an ideal occasion to create an ensemble centered on a kind of "town square," based on a principle of institutional fragmentation that he had explored in his unbuilt project of 1976 for the Jung Institute. As he admitted himself, several images haunted him at the time, in particular the paintings of Giorgio de Chirico on the theme of the piazza, and Constantin Brancusi's Paris studio, where his sculptures were placed on rough wooden bases.[2] These images informed the creation of an ensemble that evoked a miniature city, as Gehry pointed out: "I tried to build as I always do, creating a metaphor for the city with towers and turrets, old passages and strange collisions. It grows out of the stuff where I make villages."[3]

The Fritz B. Burns building, containing the classrooms, establishes the background of the composition, with a rhythm of cutouts recalling Aldo Rossi's apartment block at Gallaratese, near Milan. In the center, several flights of stairs interrupt the apparent calm. It was easy for the New York architect Henry Cobb to claim that these stairs, "when seen together with the rigorously ordered openings in the wall from which they spring, offer an eloquent metaphorical speculation on the complex and ever-problematic relationship between freedom of action and the rule of law in human society."[4]

The chapel, with its wood framework encased in glass, and the Joseph H. Donovan and Merrifield halls, both signaled by stylized columns and designed to mimic a courthouse—a key element of the school's educational practice— are responses to the rigor of the classroom building, with which these three little monuments conduct a serene conversation.

1   Notebook drawn up between November 20 and December 12, 1978. Getty Research Institute.
2   Harrison Fraker, "Spatial and Material Conventions: Frank Gehry's Artistic References," *Midgård*, vol. 1, no. 1 (1987), 105–15.
3   James W. Shields, "The Building as Village," *Reflections* (April 1989), 65.
4   Henry Cobb, preface to *The Architecture of Frank Gehry*, ed. Rosemarie Haag Bletter (New York: Rizzoli, 1986), 225.

The interior of the chapel.

Bird's-eye view showing the radial plan.

Winton Guest House

Minnesota, 1982–87

General view, with the brick chimney alcove in the foreground.

Partial view of the exterior.

The people are art collectors, and we finally made it so it appears very sculptural from the main house and all the windows are on the other side. And the building is very sculptural as you walk around it. It's made of metal, and the brown stuff is Fin-Ply—it's that formed lumber from Finland. We used it at Loyola on the chapel and it didn't work and I keep trying to make it work and in this case we learned how to detail it.

Frank Gehry, "Defending a Vision for Architecture," lecture, TED Talks, 1990.

Winton Guest House

Shoreline Drive, Wayzata, Minnesota, 1982–87
Dismantled and reassembled in 2008 on the campus of the University
of St. Thomas, Owatonna, Minnesota

In 1952, Philip Johnson built a house on the shores of Lake Minnetonka for Richard S. Davis, the director of the Minneapolis Institute of Art. The house was acquired in 1964 by Mike Winton, a construction lumber industrialist and patron of the institute. He and his wife, Penny, wanted to add a new structure to the house, for their guests. From the outset, Gehry tried to find a different language for this first house project outside of Los Angeles, as he "didn't want to mess around with Uncle Philip's baby."[1]

Gehry drew on some of his most recent projects, such as the unbuilt addition to the Smith House in Brentwood, the Benson House in Calabasas, and the theoretical Tract House project, by radicalizing the principle of fragmented volumes that characterized them. After imagining a log cabin and laying out a first compact version on an orthogonal grid, he found inspiration for their assemblage in the still lifes of Giorgio Morandi, which had been exhibited in San Francisco in 1981.[2] But one might equally make out echoes of Ellsworth Kelly's painted forms in the footprint of each element.

The six volumes that make up the house are laid out in a radial plan, pivoting around a truncated pyramid—a theme that is present in other projects of the time. They differ in height, in geometry, and especially in exterior cladding. The central space serves as a living and dining room and is finished off in painted metal. It leads directly to four other elements: a parallelepiped covered in FinPly plywood that contains the kitchen and services, with a galvanized steel box containing the bedroom for the Winton grandchildren perched on top; a brick alcove that wraps around the chimney; and two additional volumes that serve as bedrooms, with their respective bathrooms. The other volume, curvilinear in plan, sits under a half-cylinder and is clad in Kasota stone, brought in from a quarry in southern Minnesota.

A palette of muted tones similar to that used by Morandi is the final result. No window opens toward the main house, from which point the annex appears more like a large, abstract outdoor sculpture than a habitation.

Unlike the climate of southern California, the Nordic conditions in Minnesota militated against isolating one part of the structure from another, and here the junctions were ingeniously handled. The relationship between these relatively small volumes, whose uses are not rigidly fixed, is fluid and emphasized on the exterior by recessed joints where they meet. Gehry describes the introduction of "wedge-shaped cracks that serve to differentiate the parts of the pure forms and suggest that they are complete forms because of this cleavage. But in Minnesota one can imagine having snow and ice get into the cracks and that would be very difficult. We started with a very convoluted, elaborate scheme to get the water out, which seemed unnecessarily complex. Finally, when we built large-scale models we could see that the saddle detail that one would use on a normal roof was of reasonable scale so that it would not be visible, and the crack, the wedge, could still be maintained."[3]

1   Paul Goldberger, *Building Art: The Life and Work of Frank Gehry* (New York: Alfred A. Knopf, 2015), 241.
2   See Cristina Bechtler (ed.), *Frank O. Gehry/Kurt W. Forster* (Ostfildern: Cantz, 1999), 31.
3   Quoted in Pilar Viladas, "The 1980s," in Rosemarie Haag Bletter (ed.), *The Architecture of Frank Gehry* (New York: Rizzoli, 1986), 206–7.

View of the living room.

View of the living room, with one of the bedrooms visible through the window.

Bill Norton's office, overlooking the beach.

Norton House

Venice, California, 1982–84

View of the house from the Speedway looking toward the beach.

Distant view from the beach.

In this project I was dealing with the complex context of Venice. Anything you put in Venice is absorbed in about thirty seconds—nothing separates from that context. There's so much going on, so much chaos. In the Norton house, we were trying to get into that, trying to figure out how to co-opt it, how to make a piece that would be seen, have its own integrity sculpturally, and yet become part of that cacophony.

Frank Gehry, quoted in Pilar Viladas, "The 1980s," in Rosemarie Haag Bletter (ed.), *The Architecture of Frank Gehry* (New York: Rizzoli, 1986), 176.

Norton House

2509 Ocean Front Walk, Venice, California, 1982–84

Gehry has referred to this house, which is difficult to miss if one walks down Venice Beach, as his "pride and joy." Prior to this project, his work in this beachfront area of Los Angeles, where many artists had settled, had addressed different concerns. Finished off in corrugated metal, the Spiller House is located on a block at the edge of the beach. It reformulates the dialogue between wooden structure and envelope that Gehry had explored at the end of the 1970s. At some distance from the beach, a group of three cubic volumes built for Charles Arnoldi, Laddie and Guy Dill, and Bill Norton had already proposed variations on the theme of the house/studio by using three distinct exterior claddings.

Norton owned a strip of land located between the Speedway—a street accessible to vehicles—and the pedestrian promenade along the beach. He asked Gehry to build a house for his wife and artist, Lynn, and for himself, making use of an existing structure. This posed a delicate architectural problem, as the permitted construction height at the back of the building allowed for three floors, but the Nortons wished to have only one on the ocean side. This raised the risk of a certain visual imbalance. Norton reports the story of how Gehry solved the problem: "When I told him I'm a writer and need a quiet office, and that I had been a lifeguard many years before, he came up with the idea of the tower that looks out to the Pacific Ocean."[1]

The ground floor contains the studio, the bedrooms, and the garage that opens onto the back, while other rooms are located on the third floor. The living room and dining area sit between those two levels, forming a sort of *piano nobile* at the same elevation as the perch, which is accessible via an exterior stair. That extension serves as a signal toward the ocean, with its sunbreaker and the rafters projecting from its roof that evoke the unruly hair of a watchman surveying the beach.

The horizontal layering of these three levels runs counter to the linear juxtaposition of volumes that envelope them, which can be seen as a stylistic exercise in possible textures and colors. The base chords in this fanfare are provided by sky-blue tiles, which clad both the studio and the floor above. The use of glazed tiles derives from the Miriam Wosk penthouse in Beverly Hills that Gehry was building at the same time. In that project, he played with an extensive range of tiles, of every form and color, which he used to cover a linear assemblage of volumes rather similar to the Norton House. In its somewhat exhibitionist manner, the Norton House provides an effective solution to the articulation between ocean views and the intimacies of inhabitation. In the end, Gehry would come back to his initial joy. "There, I could not invent a new language: I literally used pieces of the neighboring fabric, forms and materials, to establish relationships with the city. Visually, it was satisfying, it was convincing, but I felt that it was also a compromise."[2]

1   Quoted in Mildred Friedman, *Frank Gehry: The Houses* (New York: Rizzoli, 2009), 209.
2   Quoted in Alejandro Zaera-Polo, "Conversations with Frank O. Gehry," in *Frank Gehry 1987–2003* (Madrid: El Croquis, 2006), 33.

Bill Norton's office as seen from the house.

The façade on the Speedway.

The interior staircase.

Oblique view from State Drive.

California Aerospace Museum

Los Angeles, 1982–84

General view from the south at night.

Interior with satellites suspended from the ceiling.

Interior with hanging space vehicles.

View from Main Street toward the interior plaza.

Edgemar Development

Santa Monica, 1984–88

General view from Main Street.

View from Main Street showing the superstructures.

The system I came up with was two forty-five degree angled walkways into the courtyard. And the focus of it was the elevator, which I covered in chain link, making a sculpture out of it. That was one of the San Gimignano towers. Then in the front, I put in a couple of other towers.

Frank Gehry, quoted in Mildred Friedman (ed.), *Gehry Talks: Architecture + Process* (New York: Rizzoli, 1999), 61.

Edgemar Development
2415–2449 Main Street, Santa Monica, 1984–88

Abby Sher, who lived in Santa Monica and was the daughter of a local developer, had acquired in the early 1980s a former egg factory and dairy along the Main Street commercial axis. She intended to transform one of its industrial warehouses into a contemporary art museum, financed by income from a new commercial center to be created on the site.[1] She looked to the main square of the Tuscan town of Volterra as a model, and the neighboring San Gimignano as a source for the ensemble's silhouette. This formed the basis for Frank Gehry's design, which clearly revealed his attention to urban space.

Unlike the frontal perception of the nearby Santa Monica commercial center, the buildings on Main Street are perceived at a tangent to the roadway. The most important signs are meant to be seen at a glance from a passing car, as if to echo Kevin Lynch's study of 1964, *The View from the Road*.[2] Here, references to Italian towers are combined with the culture of the billboard, although these signals do not include logos or neon signs.

The contrast between these towers and the open courts at the center of the block, which visitors reach through a maze of passageways, is a defining feature of the complex. The play between viewing it from afar and experiencing it up close, and the contrasts between the site's focal elements and its most neutral ones, derive from Gehry's readings of the classic text by Camillo Sitte, *City Building According to its Artistic Principles*, the manifesto of picturesque composition first published in the United States in 1945, and again in 1965.[3] While Gehry clearly does not share Sitte's nostalgic aesthetic, he nonetheless subscribes to the architect's critique of the spatial monotony of the modern city and his effort to recover a threatened form of sensory experience.

As a true insider, well aware of Los Angeles urban practices, Gehry would subsequently report that Sher "had fantasies about the kinds of things she liked, and they were all commercially naive." Thanks to the layout of the two passageways between boutiques located on the street—one of which was clad in turquoise tiles and featured an ice-cream vendor that had replaced the kiosk selling eggs—the visitors have the sense that there is activity inside the site and are drawn into it.

The Santa Monica Museum of Art opened in 1989 and was a victim of its own success. It ended up migrating to a larger site and was replaced by another art complex. Its neighbor, the Form Zero bookshop, relocated to the Arts District before ultimately closing its doors. Over the decades, the ensemble has been transformed, but the building volumes tangent to Main Street continue to protect the small central square. While Santa Monica Place, Gehry's remarkable interpretation of the banal shopping center program, built several blocks up north, has been disfigured, this more modest enclave has resisted the depredations of time.

1   Joseph Giovannini, "Abby Sher: Museum Founder," *The New York Times*, August 13, 1989.
2   Kevin Lynch, Donald Appleyard, and John R. Myer, *The View from the Road* (Cambridge, MA: MIT Press, 1964).
3   Camillo Sitte, *City Building According to its Artistic Principles* [1889] (New York: Random House, 1965).

The elevator enclosed in metal mesh curtains.

View of the superstructures through the metal mesh curtains surrounding the elevator.

Claes Oldenburg and Coosje van Bruggen's monumental binoculars on Main Street.

Chiat/Day Offices

Venice, California, 1985–91

General view of the three components from Main Street.

Interior view of one of the binoculars, featuring Oldenburg and van Bruggen's oversized light bulb.

So I called [Oldenburg], and I said, "I know this is a long shot: would you do the binoculars for this guy who wants them for his entry?" I said to Claes, "in order for you to do these binoculars, you have to become an architect." He said, "What does that mean?" I said, "You have to put windows in it."

Frank Gehry, quoted in Paul Goldberger, *Building Art: The Life and Work of Frank Gehry* (New York: Alfred A. Knopf, 2015), 251.

Chiat/Day Offices
340 S. Main Street, Venice, California, 1985–91

Ever since the 1960s, Gehry had assiduously frequented a phalanx of Los Angeles artists and had built houses for some of them. This office complex marks a new phase in his collaboration with sculptors, one that had begun in 1981 with the *Connections* project conceived with Richard Serra for an exhibition at the Architectural League in New York. In 1985, he designed Camp Good Times for sick children, working alongside Claes Oldenburg and Coosje van Bruggen, who were enthusiastic admirers of his 1982 house in Santa Monica. The project deployed large playful objects in a hilly landscape. Gehry also took part in the performance *Il Corso del Coltello*, which was staged by Oldenburg and van Bruggen at the Venice Biennale of 1985. The next episode in this series of collaborations unfolded in Venice, California, about half a mile from the Edgemar Development, on an L-shaped site on Main Street that had come partly into Gehry's possession as the result of a turn of events.[1] He proposed the site to Jay Chiat, an advertising executive he had recently met, who at that time was looking for a site to set up his Los Angeles offices.

The overall shape of the two wings housing the offices, the meeting rooms, and the support functions was settled upon fairly quickly. One of the wings, located parallel to the street, is partly hidden behind an open screen whose white bands evoke the decks of a ship and follow the outlines of an extended curve. The second and larger wing is laid out perpendicular to the first and ordered on the street side by a forest of rust-colored metal trees. It seemed necessary to mark the junction of these two very different volumes and to provide access to the underground parking area, but no convincing solution had been found.

After trying innumerable variations, Gehry presented a study model to Chiat in which this junction—which was reduced to a simple door—was topped provocatively by a metal box holding a roll of pins plucked from a worktable and stuck to the front of the box. The client was clearly unimpressed, but the architect changed his mind and suddenly spotted a pair of binoculars that had been used in the preparation of the *Corso del Coltello*. They had been intended for a library project in Venice, Italy. Oldenburg and van Bruggen agreed to the appropriation and developed the shape and proportions, with Gehry producing the construction plans.

With this motif—foreshadowed by the application of the F-104 Starfighter to the façade of the California Aerospace Museum—Gehry once again drew on the Los Angeles urban landscape, dotted with symbolic buildings ("ducks," in the sense used by Robert Venturi) such as the Tail O'the Pup hotdog stand or the Brown Derby restaurant in Hollywood. And like those two examples, which housed real businesses, this was not just simple décor. On its upper level, each barrel of the binoculars contains a curvilinear meeting room lit by a skylight and a giant hanging light bulb, like the image that signals the emergence of an idea in comic strips, which is meant to evoke the wellspring of creativity at the heart of the advertising agency created by Chiat and his associate, Guy Day.

1   See Paul Goldberger, *Building Art: The Life and Work of Frank Gehry* (New York: Alfred A. Knopf, 2015), 248–49.

Meeting room with Frank Gehry's bentwood chandelier.

View of the vertical fish structure.

Fish Dance Restaurant

Kobe, 1986–87

General view from the Hanshin Expressway.

The snake-shaped bar.

The fish was a kind of joke over all these references to the past. Everybody was quoting these old classical buildings, so I decided to quote something five-hundred million years older than mankind. It was also a critique on the anthropomorphism of classical architecture, by literally referring to the body of an animal. I see it more as an experiment within the architectural culture than as a significant feature of my work.

Frank Gehry, quoted in Alejandro Zaera-Polo, "Conversations with Frank O. Gehry," in *Frank Gehry 1987–2003* (Madrid: El Croquis, 2006), 39.

Fish Dance Restaurant

2 Hatobacho, Chuo Ward, Kobe, 1986–87

The emergence of the fish theme, which Gehry would explore at every scale and with the most varied textures and materials, was an expression of his visceral reaction against the historicism of postmodernism with which his name had become identified thanks to the Venice Biennale of 1980. With his taste for provocation, he proposed a return not simply to antiquity or to the Renaissance, but to the very origins of the animal kingdom. He had also reminisced many a time about his childhood in Toronto and the carps that his grandmother kept in her bathtub before cooking them up for Jewish holidays.

The monumental fish for Kobe is thus the result of several years of research. Gehry claimed that "The fish [offers] a complete vocabulary that I can draw from."[1] He was interested in interpreting the shape of the fish as a whole, to make sense of its mouth, its gill openings and its tail, and to find a way to reproduce its scales.

The edifice planted obliquely at the south end of Manhattan that Gehry proposed as part of his *Connections* project with Richard Serra took the form of a giant fish with a hook in its mouth attached by a cable to the Chrysler Building; the panels of the façade were in the shape of scales. In other projects from that time, an upright but headless fish appeared in the plan for a project in Kalamazoo that was meant to contain a hotel. Another leaped in the corner of a project for the Smith House, recalling the fountain in Jacques Tati's film *Mon Oncle*, and a fish sculpture occupied the center of a projected loft complex in New York.

Upon being contacted by the Formica company, which was looking for uses for its sheets of Colorcore laminate, Gehry proposed making box-shaped lamps but, when one prototype broke into pieces that resembled scales, the fragments were quickly reassembled into lamps and soon exhibited at the Gagosian gallery in Beverly Hills.

As these lamps were being perfected, Gehry returned to full-scale architecture with a fish-shaped building for the exhibition *Follies: Architecture for the Late Twentieth-Century Landscape*, organized by Barbara Jakobson in Leo Castelli's New York gallery. The fish was meant to house a guardian watching over a prisoner locked up inside a snake—another of Gehry's fetish forms. He subsequently created a plywood fish 12 m* long in 1985, as part of an exhibition for the Gruppo Finanziario Tessile in Florence and Turin.

Shortly thereafter, a competition for a restaurant on the quays of the port of Kobe offered him the chance to enlarge the fish motif by setting it vertically. The builder sought to create a restaurant that would be both informal and animated, so Gehry increased the size of one of his lamps to 20 m† in height, and covered it with mesh and glass scales. The fish form is accompanied by a copper-covered snake, which houses the bar, and a volume containing the grill, whose sloping roof recalls the Davis House. The fish is particularly spectacular at night, when it becomes a giant lantern illuminating the shore.

---

* 40 ft.
† 65 ft.

1 Quoted in Barbara Isenberg, *Conversations with Frank Gehry* (New York: Alfred A. Knopf, 2009), 129.

Interior view of the restaurant.

General view from the waterside.

The master bedroom and the pool.

Schnabel House

Los Angeles, 1986–89

General aerial view.

The living room, with its lead-tiled cladding.

When you say the word "deconstruction" and you look at my house, you think the term fits. But it's just an opportunistic interpretation, because it was never done intentionally. I think the Schnabel house relates to Romanesque churches I was looking at. From the outside it looks California vernacular.

Frank Gehry, quoted in Mildred Friedman (ed.), *Gehry Talks: Architecture + Process* (New York: Rizzoli, 1999), 72.

Schnabel House

526 N. Carmelina Avenue, Los Angeles, 1986–89

Built to the north of Sunset Boulevard, between a quiet residential street and a ravine carved out by an arroyo—the kind of gully that is typical of the California hills—this would be pretty much the last of Gehry's houses for some time, as larger projects were on the horizon, both in the United States and elsewhere. All the experience he had acquired with this type of program was condensed into it. The house illustrates the contamination process that characterizes the practice's work, whereby an older design can inform a new one years later, particularly through the presence of models on tables and shelves in the studio. Current projects can exchange architectural elements with older ones, sometimes very concretely, via the simple transfer of a piece of wood or cardboard from the model of one project to another.

The house was designed for Rockwell Schnabel, a businessman and Republican party figure turned diplomat, who served under Ronald Reagan's second administration as ambassador to Finland. Schnabel's wife, Marna, had worked in Gehry's office, where she had built the model of the Tract House for an exhibition at the Leo Castelli gallery. The compact construction of 2,700 sq. ft.* that brought together several separate volumes was proposed as an alternative to the repetitive houses in the subdivisions of southern California. Although the gallery project was soon abandoned, Marna remained passionate about the proposition. Gregory Walsh reports that she told him, "I'll get a lot, and I'll ask [Gehry] to build it."[1] A subsequent attempt to enlarge the compact configuration of the Tract House did not measure up to the Schnabels' ambitious program, and the plan took on the form of a village instead; its central element—by its location a sort of equivalent to a church—is the volume of the cruciform living room, whose wooden structure is covered in lead tiles. Once again, Gehry took advantage of the freedom provided by the wood frame to create a space flooded with natural light.

Planted in the middle of the plot, the living area reprises a form considered at one time for the Winton House, which provides room for a front garden and a swimming pool running along the side. The ambassador's study sits in the middle of the garden, housed in a volume finished off in white, with a copper sphere on top, evoking both the globe placed on top of the Aerospace Museum and the onion domes of Orthodox churches that reminded him of Finland's Russian past.

The other elements of the dwelling are laid out further back on the site, starting with the kitchen and service wing, in a long building pushed close to the property line as an extension to the garage. The site's natural slope is ingeniously employed: the main bedroom is placed at a lower level than the rest of the house, surrounded by a pool that overlooks the arroyo. On top of the bedroom sits a belvedere, designed in the same spirit as the metal forest screening the Chiat/Day building.

---

*   250 sq. m

1   Quoted in Mildred Friedman (ed.), *Gehry Talks: Architecture + Process* (New York: Rizzoli, 1999), 205.

View of the master bedroom.

View of the living room.

Exterior view showing a spiral staircase.

Vitra Design Museum

Weil am Rhein, 1987–89

View from Römerstrasse.

Partial view of the exterior.

I was interested in the play between my building
and Nicholas Grimshaw's earlier high-tech factory,
and I didn't want to preempt Grimshaw's high-techness.
I thought it was good that he maintained that, and
that I should either go way out forward or, well, I didn't
have the money to go way out forward with the factory,
so I just cut big holes in the walls, and it looked like
an old-fashioned factory. When it was built, the factory
part looked like it was there before Grimshaw's.

Frank Gehry, quoted in Mildred Friedman (ed.), *Gehry Talks: Architecture + Process* (New York: Rizzoli, 1999), 97.

Vitra Design Museum
Charles-Eames-Strasse 2, Weil am Rhein, 1987–89

This little building, located on the border between Germany and the Swiss canton of Basel, was not just Gehry's European debut, following the unfruitful competitions for the Nîmes media center and the Bicocca neighborhood of Milan, but it was also a spatial and aesthetic inflexion point in his work. Vitra produces the furniture designed by Charles and Ray Eames for Herman Miller. In the New York studio of Claes Oldenburg and Coosje van Bruggen, Gehry met its president, Rolf Fehlbaum, who had just commissioned a sculpture from them that could serve as a landmark and gate to the factories; this work would turn out to be *Balancing Tools*, created in 1984.[1]

A fire had destroyed the original factory in 1981, and Nicholas Grimshaw had designed new hangars to replace it. As the initial commission for a "small shelter" for Fehlbaum's collection of chairs, which was his first idea, was not financially remunerative enough, Gehry was asked to provide an additional industrial building and a museum. The latter became a sort of pavilion placed in front of the rectangular volume of the factory, which serves as a backdrop, with spiral staircases pinned to it as decoration. It was as if Robert Venturi's concept of the dichotomy between the "decorated shed" and the "duck" had become a reality, through the encounter between the first element (the factory) and the second (the museum), with its strange shape. Gehry paid close attention to establishing the correct relationship between the two; as he put it, "I was playing with something that I was interested in, which was the urban quality that I could create out in that field, the urban quality between the museum and those entrances."[2]

The conundrum that Gehry faced was how to achieve the formal freedom that he had attained through the use of wood frames in California while employing European construction techniques. Some buildings relatively close by, such as Rudolf Steiner's Goetheanum in Dornach and Le Corbusier's chapel at Ronchamp, logically came to mind. He was also familiar with the cubo-futurist compositions of Lyubov Popova and Alexander Vesnin.

At this point, the process of deconstructing volumes that had given rise to most of Gehry's projects since the 1970s came to term. Here they would be integrated into a fluid continuum, unified visually by their white exterior coating and their zinc roofs, which were commonly used in the region's vernacular industrial buildings. The spiral form of the stairs—the first twisting shapes to appear in Gehry's work—created a contrast with the prismatic galleries. This sculptural play that introduces unity through diversity is further heightened by the contrast between the structure and the green lawns that surround it.

Vitra would continue this approach by creating a collection of edifices designed by Zaha Hadid, Tadao Ando, Alvaro Siza, and Herzog & de Meuron. Gehry worked on an extension to the museum in 1998 but it remains unbuilt. However, between 1988 and 1994 he would design a small building in Birsfelden, on the opposite bank of the Rhine, for Fehlbaum's offices, whose animated volume indicates the new directions in which the Vitra project had launched him.

1 Paul Goldberger, *Building Art: The Life and Work of Frank Gehry* (New York: Alfred A. Knopf, 2015), 252.
2 Quoted in Mildred Friedman (ed.), *Gehry Talks: Architecture + Process* (New York: Rizzoli, 1999), 97.

Interior views of the galleries.

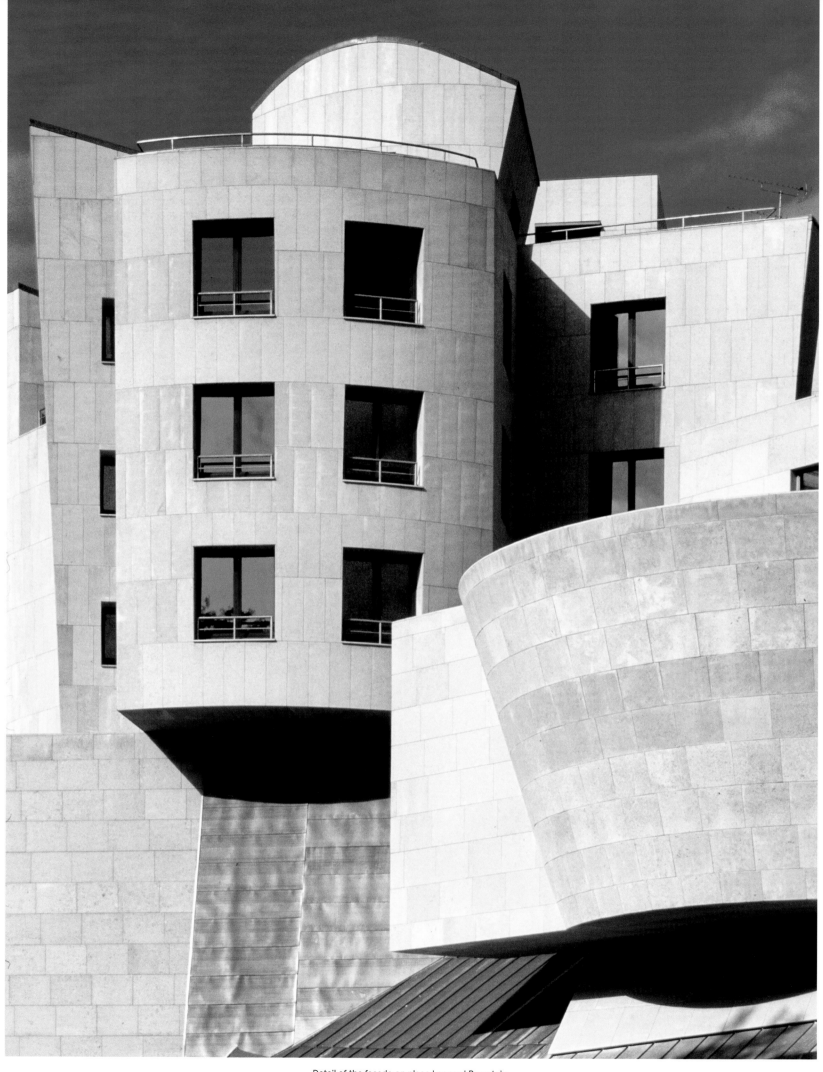

Detail of the façade on place Leonard Bernstein.

American Center – Cinémathèque Française

Paris, 1988–94

General view from the Parc de Bercy.

I wanted the project to be a *petite ville*, just like the city, full of music, activity, and energy. I tried to make the central place an open space, so that from there you could go to the movie theater, the main theater, the restaurant, and you would have been able to go into the book shop and travel agency. Then the loft made sense as a kind of living room sitting in the middle of the space. The gallery is way up to the top, because that was the only place I could put it to get top light.

Frank Gehry, quoted in Mildred Friedman (ed.), *Gehry Talks: Architecture + Process* (New York: Rizzoli, 1999), 111.

View of the main staircase.

View of the side façade on rue Paul Belmondo.

American Center – Cinémathèque Française
51 rue de Bercy, Paris, 1988–94

More than twenty-five years after a life-changing stay in Paris, Gehry had the opportunity to return with flying colors when the American Center decided to abandon the neoclassical building erected in 1934 on boulevard Raspail by William Welles Bosworth and relocate to a site adjacent to the new park at Bercy. At the time, he was working on a commercial and entertainment center at the entrance to the Disneyland theme park in Marne-la-Vallée, which was causing him to reflect on symbolic and playful architecture. There would be none of that in his building for the American Center, where he saw the chance to use some of the textures of Haussmann's Paris, such as stone-clad façades and zinc rooftops, as a challenge.

The center was intended not only to rehouse the facilities on boulevard Raspail, but also to bring together its various activities. The program therefore focused on largely public disciplines—theater, cinema, exhibitions, and performances—but it also included more intimate work places, along with accommodations for visitors. From the outset, it was conceived as different from any simple residential building, office building, or theater, an approach that suggested an assemblage, a negotiation between the different uses. Gehry's experience in this area enabled him to obtain the commission over the other competitors, who included Richard Meier.

The design process was rather complex. Budget constraints led to a brutal compression of the facilities that had been distributed rather generously around the main hall in the initial versions. Over the following months, changing interpretations of urban regulations and increasingly precise financial projections led to several reformulations of the basic project, not only in its dimensions, but also in its very makeup. But as the different building volumes became more distinct, it was also possible to fix the interior spaces more firmly. The entrance, located at a turn in the road that leads to the park, was transformed into a vertical combination of sloping prisms with echoes of the California Aerospace Museum, while the glass carapace turned into a series of screens detached from the façade.

The impression of a gradual combination of separate elements that had characterized the first versions gave way to the vertical development of a continuous surface: the wall is sometimes interrupted to allow circulation elements at the ground floor to pass through it, and it registers the changing nature of the interior activities on the upper floors. While on the whole the façade is simple cladding, this skin sometimes peels back from the building and curls back on itself to take on a specific sculptural quality, all without blocking daylight from the windows. The different sides of the building contrast markedly with each other: dynamic and vibrating at the corner near the park, more well behaved where the façade envelops the apartments, and ultimately calm and restrained where it clads the auditorium on the east, with the ancillary space of the backstage area more akin to the mews that service the rear of buildings in Los Angeles.

The building remained unoccupied for some time following the bankruptcy of the American Center but was taken over in 2005 by the Cinémathèque Française, which was able to insert screening rooms with ease and to use the galleries for its temporary exhibitions.

View from the garden terrace.

Walt Disney Concert Hall

Los Angeles, 1988–2003

Bird's-eye view with Grand Avenue.

View of the lobby and the stairs leading to the parking garage.

The architecture of Disney Hall doesn't get in the way of people walking in and out. It's inviting. Accessibility is a big priority in all my work. The key issue is to know what does the building say to the people on the street, how does it welcome them? I don't think that destroys or negates an artist's position. I want people to be able to interact with my ideas and not to be intimidated by them. This is very important, particularly today. I also think there is a freer spirit here on this site in Los Angeles: there is no context to speak of and we build in the middle of nowhere. This allows for a much freer expression. I wanted this building to be one idea, inside and outside, one aesthetic, unlike traditional concert halls. I wanted it to express the joy and feeling of music.

Frank Gehry, quoted in Mark Rappolt and Robert Violette (eds.), *Gehry Draws* (Cambridge, MA: MIT Press/Violette Editions, 2004), 312.

Walt Disney Concert Hall

111 S. Grand Avenue, Los Angeles, 1988–2003

No one is a prophet in his or her own city. Gehry had learned this lesson after being sidelined from the commissions for the Los Angeles Museum of Contemporary Art and for the Getty Center, and when multiple obstacles contrived to block his way for fifteen years before he was able to complete the Walt Disney Concert Hall. Gehry had been invited to compete for the project, along with Gottfried Böhm, Hans Hollein, and James Stirling, and in 1988 he obtained the commission for a new cultural institution that Lillian Disney had just donated fifty million dollars to the city to pay for.

The location selected for the project was a site on Bunker Hill, previously a crowded, impoverished neighborhood demolished by postwar urban renewal that overlooked the dense center of Los Angeles, its grid interrupted by the Hollywood Freeway. First Street separated the site from the Music Center, the local version of New York's Lincoln Center, built by Welton Becket.

In the initial competition project, the concert hall, in the form of a stepped pyramid clad in stone, was combined with a metal grid structure intended for the foyer and access points. Chain link, which Gehry had often used in Los Angeles, was quickly rejected as an option. A variant completely draped in limestone, with double-curved walls, was also considered, but the poor aging of the exterior of the American Center in Paris discredited this approach. Over the course of the design, as the size of the program grew significantly, the idea of a metal exterior envelope gained ground, first as a part of the cladding, and later as a covering for all the volumes under consideration.

On the recommendation of Ernest Fleischmann, the director of the Los Angeles Philharmonic and one of the hall's future users, Gehry studied the Berliner Philharmonie in detail, which he found to be close to his own approach: "You get a lot of similarities by following the rules of the game. It's not that I copied Hans Scharoun. It's that the game was the same, and the client asked for the same diagram."[1] The acoustician Yasuhisa Toyota shared his admiration for the hall in Berlin, and they immediately understood each other. In the end, the 2,265-seat auditorium, with its extravagant display of organ pipes that Gehry designed, was much appreciated for its musical qualities.

On the outside, Gehry would have loved to have intervened in the neighborhood, but extending beyond the project boundaries was out of the question. So he responded only to those buildings that were immediately adjacent: "I took the curve of the [Dorothy] Chandler [Pavilion] and broke down the scale of Disney Hall so as not to disrupt the iconic preeminence of Chandler. I didn't want to because of a social commitment that goes back to the 1960's. I tried to make it better by what I did."[2] On account of refinements to the metal skin, which benefited from a long pause in the design process (the budget had skyrocketed), and lessons drawn from Bilbao, the enclosure of the main hall, the circulation spaces, and the vestibules were reduced in size, but this would be compensated for by access to exterior terraces during intermissions.

The interruption in the design work also made it possible to fully integrate the use of CATIA computer-aided design software into both the monument's conception and its construction. The hall remained isolated for a long time but is now in the company of the Broad Museum and is awaiting the completion of an office and commercial complex by Gehry (2020–22) on the opposite side of Grand Avenue.

1   Quoted in Mildred Friedman (ed.), *Gehry Talks: Architecture + Process* (New York: Rizzoli, 1999), 149.
2   Frank Gehry, interview with the author (Los Angeles, July 2000).

The organ pipes in the auditorium.

The auditorium as seen from the balcony level.

View of the exterior at dusk.

Weisman Art Museum

Minneapolis, 1990–93

General view from the west bank of the Mississippi.

We'd just worked on the American Center in Paris, where we started to introduce that kind of curve. Also, if you look at my drawings, you can see that I was thinking about Tibetan monasteries and how they looked on the hillside. When you approached the site from the Minneapolis side by bridge, it reminded me of the monasteries. It was very high from the floor level of the building down to the riverbed, maybe a couple hundred feet, maybe more. I had a façade facing the river, and that's what I started drawing.

Frank Gehry, quoted in Barbara Isenberg, *Conversations with Frank Gehry* (New York: Alfred A. Knopf, 2009), 87.

View from the south.

View from Washington Avenue.

Weisman Art Museum

333 E. River Road, Minneapolis, 1990–93

Frederick R. Weisman had made an immense fortune importing Toyota automobiles into the United States. He turned to Frank Gehry in 1978 to build an important office complex in Maryland. With his wife, Marcia Simon, he had become one of the most important supporters of contemporary art on the West Coast, to the point of inspiring David Hockney's painting of 1968, *American Collectors*. Having already commissioned several projects from Gehry in Los Angeles, he turned to the university in his native city of Minneapolis and proposed to finance a new building for his art museum, which since 1934 had occupied temporary quarters. After a brief competition against rivals Arata Isozaki, Cesar Pelli, and Machado & Silvetti, Gehry obtained the commission.

The site chosen for the project was spectacular. Located on the crest of a cliff overlooking the Mississippi valley, offering a panoramic view of the center of Minneapolis, it signaled the western access point to the university campus from Washington Avenue. The contrast between orthogonal factory box and lyrical museum, represented by two separate buildings in the Vitra project and the California Aerospace Museum, is here superseded in favor of a hybrid, dual form, in which a volume inspired (according to Gehry) by Tibetan monasteries becomes the bowsprit to a solid parallelepiped attached to a road bridge. To return once more to the agonistic terms identified by Robert Venturi, the "duck" is brought in to decorate the "shed."

The principal galleries are contained in the main section of the building. Their rectangular forms in plan are contradicted, so to speak, by the play of the roofs, which flood them with natural light reflected on curved surfaces. The effects that were carefully limited at Vitra are now multiplied and work with the structural beams bursting in, sheathed in plaster like those at the Los Angeles Temporary Contemporary (1983). This illustrates an original feature of Gehry's architecture: his imaginative design of ceilings, which in other contemporary museums are often treated as simple surfaces equipped with light fixtures.

The break introduced by this project stems from the modeling of the figurehead at the prow—a sophisticated play of forms and counter-forms that creates an animated surface housing small galleries and offices. After considering cladding it in copper, Gehry decided to use thin plates of stainless steel, curved so as to reproduce the shapes he developed in the model. He justified the choice of this material and its shiny finish on the basis of local conditions: "We went with the shiny finish for the Weisman museum because of the light in Minneapolis."[1] Defining the shape of each of these plates required a considerable amount of work in the office, which pushed the team to introduce computerized methods of design and production as soon as possible.

An extension designed by the Gehry office in 2011 running the length of the east façade holds several square galleries and a workshop for collaborative projects. It is clad in brick, like the main section of the museum, and has made the view from the campus more pleasant.

---

1   Quoted in Mildred Friedman (ed.), *Gehry Talks: Architecture + Process* (New York: Rizzoli, 1999), 150.

Interior view of one of the galleries.

View from Iparraguirre Kalea, with Jeff Koons's *Puppy*.

Guggenheim Museum

Bilbao, 1991–97

Aerial view of the site from the west.

View of the atrium from below.

I like the idea of going to a museum, seeing a section of it, then coming back to the center. You could branch out again, as well as be able to go in a continuous fashion around the central space. In this case, I also wanted to have the central space open to the city so that whenever you came back to that central space open to the city, you had different views of Bilbao around you. It made the experience interactive and seeing art interacting with the city made sense to me.

Frank Gehry, quoted in Barbara Isenberg, *Conversations with Frank Gehry* (New York: Alfred A. Knopf, 2009), 138.

How do you make a big monolithic building that's humane? I try to fit into the city. In Bilbao I took on the bridge, the river, and the road, and I tried to make a building that was scaled to the nineteenth-century city.

Frank Gehry, quoted in Paul Goldberger, *Building Art: The Life and Work of Frank Gehry* (New York: Alfred A. Knopf, 2015), 291.

View of the ground-floor gallery, featuring Richard Serra's *Snake*.

Guggenheim Museum
Abandoibarra Etorbidea 2, Bilbao, 1991–97

When in 2005 *Vanity Fair* asked some fifty experts what they considered
to be the most memorable building constructed since 1980, the Bilbao
museum came out the clear winner. Hadn't Philip Johnson already claimed,
in comparing it to Chartres Cathedral, that it was "the greatest building of
our time"?[1]

This undertaking began with an agreement between Thomas Krens,
the director of the Guggenheim Museum in New York, and the Basque
government to create a branch in the regional capital. In 1991, Gehry was
consulted as to its placement and rejected the initial location in the city
center in favor of a new building in the valley of the Nervión river, which
was lined with abandoned steel factories. Unlike the sketches provided for
the new site by his competitors Arata Isozaki and Coop Himmelb(l)au, he
responded empathetically to the site conditions, saying, "I was responding
to the bridge, the toughness of the waterfront, its industrial character."[2]

Over the course of the following months, the project took shape through
close interplay between study models and sketches, with early orthogonal
forms gradually replaced by a continuum of curved forms, in a process
that Gehry compares to skating: "Everything connected with everything
else seems freer, not taking your hands off. I love the free flow."[3] The shape
of a snake, which was present for a good while, was put aside, while other
sources, such as Giovanni Bellini's painting *Madonna with Child* that Gehry
saw at the National Gallery in London, inspired the relationship between
the volumes. A hierarchy emerged between the main atrium—the pivot
point of the museum—and the galleries, the largest of which, curved in
on itself, began more and more to resemble a fish.

The lead-coated copper originally projected for the exterior was replaced
by titanium, which had become more affordable after the collapse of the
Soviet aeronautical industry. But the execution of the project required fifty
thousand drawings and radical changes in the office's working methods,
including the introduction of CATIA software, created by aeronautical
engineers at Dassault. It took more than sixty thousand hours to digitize
the physical model and to produce representations that could be used to
calculate and fabricate both the structure and the cladding panels, and that
could be transmitted directly to the contractors.

Inside the atrium, which invites comparisons to Frank Lloyd Wright's
design for the Guggenheim in New York, the suspended pathways are
not used for the installation of artworks, as in Wright's version. Instead,
they afford glimpses of the large vertical forms that mark the rhythm of
the space as well as views of the city, and they lead from gallery to gallery.
In accordance with Krens's wishes, the galleries that display artworks lent
by the Guggenheim are orthogonal volumes, completely conventional and
indifferent to their content. They are complemented by individually shaped
galleries that house artworks specifically created for installation *in situ*,
by Sol LeWitt, Anselm Kiefer, and others. The ground-floor gallery running
along the river was laid out around the *Snake*, a work commissioned specially
from Richard Serra, who would end up not being particularly grateful to
Gehry. The museum was a turning point for its architect, and it marked an
important threshold in the concept of museums and their place in the city.

1   Matt Tyrnauer, "Architecture in the Age of Gehry," *Vanity Fair*, June 30, 2010.
2   Quoted in Coosje van Bruggen, *Frank O. Gehry: Guggenheim Museum Bilbao* (New York: Guggenheim Publications, 1998), 33.
3   Ibid., 37.

Detail of the façade, with the glass envelope of the atrium.

View from the Nervión river.

View from Jirásek Square.

Nationale-Nederlanden Building

Prague, 1992–96

General view across the Vltava, with the Jirásek bridge.

The building at night, with its cupola lit up.

My perception was that in Prague they designed the old buildings with implied towers. They put little caps on top of them and gave them each a hat. That was interesting to me. That was a clue. The other was that in the nineteenth century, the windows and other elements had details that gave a certain texture to the buildings. Even though they looked like they were stone all the buildings were colored plaster. I picked up clues from the plaster, and from whatever I saw.

Frank Gehry, quoted in Mildred Friedman (ed.), *Gehry Talks: Architecture + Process* (New York: Rizzoli, 1999), 207.

Nationale-Nederlanden Building
Jiráskovo Náměstí 1981/6, Nové Město, Prague, 1992–96

The fall of the Berlin Wall and the collapse of the Socialist bloc opened up new horizons for Frank Gehry from 1992 onward. In Prague, he was invited to design a building on a site that had remained vacant since the bombings of World War II, located at the end of the Jirásek bridge, on the docks of the right bank of the Vltava. Following the Velvet Revolution of 1989, President Václav Havel had asked the architect Vlado Milunić to build an art gallery on the site. But the Dutch bank ING ended up purchasing the plot with the intention of constructing an office building. It decided to award the commission to an internationally famous architect. Gehry accepted the invitation and began to prepare designs in association with Milunić, who helped him discover some of the particularities of Prague's urban landscape.

After drawing a sort of elephant rising up over the square in his initial sketches, Gehry had the idea of combining two towers, originally cylindrical in shape, one serving as a ball joint at the angle where the quay meets the square, and the other facing it. He imagined cladding the second tower in glass, and his sketches show that he later pinched it in the middle and twisted it round, along the lines of the vertical volumes of the Bilbao atrium. Its combination with the corner tower, which had remained basically cylindrical, inevitably brings to mind the giant pair of knees that Claes Oldenburg had drawn up in 1966 for the Victoria Embankment in London, a site in some ways comparable in its relation to the river. A plaster model of Gehry's seems to be directly derived from it. CATIA software made it possible to develop a buildable form from the large number of exploratory sketches.

The movement of the glazed tower—and the exterior cladding cut off at ground-floor level, resembling a calf-length skirt—inspired Milunić to compare it to the actress and dancer Ginger Rogers. Gehry subsequently called the other, more masculine tower Fred Astaire, in homage to their on-screen partnership during the 1930s and 1940s.

But the building recalls not only the mythical figures of Hollywood—a reference that became quite popular but also scandalized the local critics. The joyous lines of the façade along the quay, which is lined with some of the best buildings of the Prague Secession, resonate—as Gehry put it—with the "nineteenth-century texture" of the city, and "its finesse." The variation of the window heights produces an undulating effect that extends the effect created by motifs on adjacent buildings, whose moldings are echoed in the projecting metal window frames. Beyond eclectic or Secessionist themes, even a little Czech baroque comes through as well.

Another echo of the urban landscape of Prague, which Gehry examined very closely in the early phases of the project, is the cupola that reflects the domes on top of other buildings in the city. It is built from a steel skeleton holding bands of metal, and a number of metal flourishes project from the openwork. The textures of southern California thus appear among the rooftops of the Czech capital in such a tousled and disheveled state that Gehry declared he had come to see the object as an allusion to Medusa.

View of the skirt-shaped form of the "Ginger" glass tower.

General view from the harbor.

Neuer Zollhof

Düsseldorf, 1994–99

Aerial view of the site, with the Rhine behind.

The metal-clad central building.

I was trying to fit into the urban pattern and leave the river front open so that the people behind would have a view to the river. All the buildings being built so far have been built as a wall against the river. So all the people behind are being walled off from the river. We decided not to do that.... It represents the new world we're in. There's more individuality. It's about democracy.

Frank Gehry, quoted in Mildred Friedman (ed.), *Gehry Talks: Architecture + Process* (New York: Rizzoli, 1999), 228.

Neuer Zollhof
Neuer Zollhof 2–6, Düsseldorf, 1994–99

With his three office buildings for the Neuer Zollhof—or New Customs House—built on the edge of the Rhine in Düsseldorf, Gehry's working principles for achieving unity in diversity are of another order than in the Stata Center (see pp. 236–45), because here it was a question not of how to divide up an integrated structure, but of creating affinities between isolated elements whose functions are fairly simple.

The complex forms part of the conversion of the largest river port in Germany, which for a long time was the outlet for the Ruhr, into a new quarter devoted to information technology companies and audiovisual production, the Media Harbour. Between 1989 and 1993, as the result of a competition, Zaha Hadid had laid out a Media Park for this site that formed a continuous landscape that was to house the various programs. But the project's prohibitive cost resulted in its being abandoned, and the commission for a more limited version was passed on to Gehry, who had been in contact for some time previously with the client, Thomas Rempen.

The ground plate for this ensemble of spaces for communication, advertisement, and insurance companies is located on the banks of the river. A residential quarter runs alongside it to the south, while the center of the city lies to the east, not far from the parliament building for North Rhine-Westphalia, laid out at the end of the 1880s on a circular plan. Unlike the two neighboring ensembles, which form a vertical wall at the water, the basic massing of the Zollhof preserves views toward the river from the Wupperstrasse and the Lippestrasse, which link it to the neighborhoods to the south. The relationship between the city and the river, rather than being blocked or denied, is instead enriched by perspectives framed between Gehry's buildings, which focus on this aspect of proximity, just like a camera lens.

According to Craig Webb, one of the authors of the project, the composition echoes a painting by Giovanni Bellini in which the Virgin Mary and the infant Jesus (the building in the middle) are framed by Saints Joseph and John the Baptist (the buildings to either side).[1] There are several orders of affinity between the three isolated buildings. They are all conceived according to the same pyramidal principle, with the dominant central piece flanked by lower volumes that seem almost like tentacles in plan. Inside the volumes, the spaces are laid out as open-plan offices or with modular interior partitions, depending on the needs of the users. Maximum advantage is taken of the views to the river and the city by locating circulation elements and services at the junctions of the concave façades, the better for diffusing daylight along the edges.

The buildings are clad in three different skins, while the prefabricated concrete panels required by the construction teams were individually poured in molds shaped using CATIA software and are invisible from the outside. The unity of the project is established not by the materials used on the façades, which are all different, but by the fact that they all share the same kind of form, and by the repetition—independent of the treatment of the façades—of metal doors and windows, which are set at different angles, a feature that militates against their serial repetition.

The center building, the lowest of the three, is covered in reflective metal, shaped to accentuate the vertical rhythm. The highest one is coated in white, whereas the third is faced in brick, the vernacular material for factories and warehouses in what was previously one of the most powerful industrial regions in Europe.

---

1   Quoted in Mark Rappolt and Robert Violette (eds.), *Gehry Draws* (Cambridge, MA: MIT Press/Violette Editions, 2004), 190.

View looking east toward the Rhine, with the brick-clad building at left.

The façade on Pariser Platz.

DZ Bank Building

Berlin, 1995–2001

The glazed atrium and the metal envelope of the meeting room.

I obey the golden rule. I think that the big issue is to be a good neighbor. That means that you respect what's around you and its context. It's again the [Erich] Mendelsohn lesson, that you relate to it, that you bring something to it that wasn't there but it's part of. I have tried to do that here in relationship with the Brandenburg Gate, which is large, stony; it has a certain toughness and a certain character, and I gave to the façade on Pariser Platz a character that would not detract or would not trivialize the Brandenburg Gate.

Frank O. Gehry, "Building at the Pariser Platz, Facets of a Challenge," lecture given in Berlin, 2000, typewritten transcript, 3. Gehry Partners.

Night view from Pariser Platz, with the Brandenburg Gate.

DZ Bank Building
Pariser Platz 3, Berlin, 1995–2001

At the same time as he was working on the project in Prague, Gehry was getting to know another site that bore the wounds of World War II: the Pariser Platz, where the Brandenburg Gate marks the end of the monumental axis of Unter den Linden. But, this time, developing a sculptural interpretation of the landscape of the newly relocated capital was out of the question. Nor was it really possible to draw inspiration from the dynamic undulations of Erich Mendelsohn's Einstein Tower in Potsdam. According to Gehry, the tower could be understood only "in context."

The Berlin Senate insisted that specific construction heights be respected and that the building should conform to the rigid straight lines of the square. This did not preclude searching for a design that contrasted with the two neighboring buildings, the Akademie der Künste and the embassy of the United States. So Gehry found himself "playing by the rules" while avoiding literal imitation. He set himself the task of somehow capturing the "sense of the place" and respecting it, of "not being disrespectful" of it, recognizing that "the city [has] a language invested by the inhabitants" and that "as an *Ausländer*, a visitor, you have to understand it." The north façade, behind which are the offices of the Deutsche Zentral-Genossenschaftsbank, sits on the edge of the square and is therefore sensibly composed of large rectangular bays arranged as if on parade, whereas the elevation of the dwelling units on the south side undulates freely. And in another effort on Gehry's part to be contextual, both façades are made up of massive blocks of a limestone similar to that used on the Brandenburg Gate.

While working on the initial project, Gehry found himself short on ideas for the conference hall requested by the bank, and he improvised by recycling an element of one of the many models made over the years for the Peter Lewis House in Lyndhurst, Ohio. Its shape, evoking a horse's head, lent itself to the elongated space of the covered atrium. The hall's particularly slow gestation was marked in 1993 by Gehry's discovery, in the company of the historian Irving Lavin, of the mourners sculpted by Claus Sluter in Dijon at the beginning of the fifteenth century for the tomb of Philip the Bold.[1] The overall form of their hoods and their supple outlines struck Gehry on account of their resemblance to his model, and his observations helped him refine the design of the conference hall. After exploring a multitude of different possibilities, the interior of the final version is finished off with a warm wood, while the exterior form of the volume, clad in thin metal plates, seems to be trying to push back the boundary of the atrium.

The horse's head is thus both container and contained, covered as it is by a spidery glazed structure, designed by the Stuttgart engineer Jörg Schlaich, that contrasts with the wooden panels of the interior façade. This composite block, which is discreet on the side facing the square and more eloquent on the Behrenstrasse, which separates it from the Memorial to the Murdered Jews of Europe, designed by Peter Eisenman, reformulates the duality frequently found in Gehry's work between serial, repetitive elements and a sculptural component—with the latter in this case interiorized and undetectable from the outside.

---

1   Irving Lavin, "Going for Baroque: Frank Gehry and the Post-Modern Drapery Fold," in *Frank Gehry: 1987–2003* (Madrid: El Croquis, 2006), 42.

The interior of the meeting room.

View of the west façade.

Experience Music Project

Seattle, 1995–2000

Bird's-eye view from the Space Needle.

Exterior view from 5th Avenue.

I'm still interested in objects in a field, like villages, but I don't see that idea rigidly applied. I think you can see it in the Experience Music Project, where I started out with separate blocks that the client, Paul Allen, liked. That's the village. If you look at the first models, I was making it more coherent. He didn't like it. He liked the models when I broke it down. I did too, actually. And when I broke it apart, I liked what was going on. I didn't achieve it in that model. Essentially, the building is a one-room warehouse with exhibits inside, and that makes it difficult to break down.

Frank Gehry, quoted in Mildred Friedman (ed.), *Gehry Talks: Architecture + Process* (New York: Rizzoli, 1999), 237.

Experience Music Project
325 5th Avenue N., Seattle, 1995–2000

In 1995, while construction of the Bilbao museum was under way, Frank Gehry was approached by Paul Allen, the co-founder of Microsoft. Since his retirement, Allen had become one of the most generous philanthropists in North America. He was passionate about rock music and was a fan of Jimi Hendrix, who was born, like he was, in Seattle. Allen sought to "capture the exuberance of [his] music in a building" that would tell Hendrix's story and reproduce the atmosphere of his sound. In clarifying his intentions, he would later state, "I came up with the term 'swoopy.' I wanted the feeling of colorful, psychedelic art."[1]

The site is located outside the city, on the grounds of the Seattle World's Fair of 1962. Its main landmark, John Graham's Space Needle, towers over it, and another vestige of the event, the elevated tracks of the Seattle Center Monorail, cut through the new building.

In response to Allen's expectations, Gehry strove to create an *architecture parlante*: a type of architecture that speaks (or, rather, makes sounds). To do so, he had to familiarize himself with Hendrix's music, which he had never much enjoyed. Knowing that the singer used to like smashing up his electric guitars on stage, he started buying instruments by Fender, such as the famous Stratocaster, which he broke into pieces, seeking inspiration by reassembling their fragments. Gehry's design could also be compared to John Chamberlain's crumpled sheet metal or César's compressions. Planning the relationship between the building's constituent parts, he drew on the research he conducted for years for the Lewis House; as in that project, their proximity recalls objects in the paintings of Giorgio Morandi.

The building's logic combines both a principle of fragmentation and a principle of confluence. The six separate exterior volumes are connected over the course of a visit, which unfolds fluidly inside the cavernous spaces and ties them one to another, with access via canyons that extend throughout from the two entrances.

The section known as the "Artist's Journey" is separated from the five others by the monorail, which affords a passing view of the interior, finished in blue-colored aluminum. It presents the lives of musicians and their historical context over the course of a narrative rich in biographical episodes. On the other side of the tracks, the "Sky Church," with its purple skin, derives from an idea suggested by Hendrix himself: that of a concert hall in which even the most varied audiences could commune thanks to the power of music, whether they were listeners or were playing it themselves.

The other thematic spaces are the "Crossroad," where all the currents in American pop music come together, and the "Sound Lab," a place where all audiences can learn music, which is equipped with state-of-the-art technology. In the same informative and popular spirit, the "Electric Library" and the "Education House" contain multimedia archives and teaching and play programs geared to local user groups.

Locally, the building met with incomprehension. As for the critic of *The New York Times*, Herbert Muschamp, who was generally supportive of Gehry, he described it with a certain malice as less a collage of guitars than "something that crawled out of the sea, rolled over, and died."[2] A Science Fiction Museum and Hall of Fame were created inside the initial volumes in 2004, and in 2016 the Experience Music Project, which by that time occupied a reduced space, was rechristened "MoPOP" (Museum of Pop Culture).

1   Quoted in Paul Goldberger, *Building Art: The Life and Work of Frank Gehry* (New York: Alfred A. Knopf, 2015), 326.
2   Herbert Muschamp, "Architecture: The Library That Puts on Fishnets and Hits the Disco," *The New York Times*, May 16, 2004.

View of the interior and the main stairs.

Side view of the main entrance.

Richard B. Fisher Center, Bard College

Annandale-on-Hudson, New York, 1997–2003

Evening view.

Oblique view of the main façade.

It's modest. If you straightened all that stuff out, if you made a box out of this whole, you'd save about a million and a half dollars, less than ten per cent of the total cost. But that's always the case. The "decoration" I call it, whatever we do as architects, is usually less than ten per cent of the building.... The materials are as cheap as we can build it. The main box of the building is concrete and it will be exposed both outside and inside; the panels are acoustically molded. The balconies are wood and the acoustical shell, where the orchestra sits, is wood. That will make it pleasant. But it's not expensive, it's not fancy.

Frank Gehry, quoted in Mildred Friedman (ed.), *Gehry Talks: Architecture + Process* (New York: Rizzoli, 1999), 266.

Richard B. Fisher Center, Bard College

Manor Avenue, Annandale-on-Hudson, New York, 1997–2003

Before starting on the lengthy undertaking that would culminate in the Disney Concert Hall, Gehry had already gained extensive experience with spaces devoted to music by way of his projects for the Hollywood Bowl and the pavilions in Columbia, Maryland, and in Concord, California, conceived in collaboration with the acoustician Christopher Jaffe.

A new opportunity came to him via the president of Bard College, an institution located in the Hudson Valley, a two-hour drive north of New York, where the curriculum revolves around music and theater. Leon Botstein, the principal conductor of the American Symphony Orchestra, invited Gehry to design a facility for public concerts, theater performances, and for training students on the wooded campus not far from the schools for art, dance, and music.

A nearby industrial building inspired Gehry to imagine a heterogeneous structure in two "languages," combining a pile of orthogonal volumes and a great metallic rumple, which he has compared to a handkerchief. He claims that "the front façade of the building can be interpreted as a theatrical mask that covers the raw face of the performance space. Its abstract forms prepare the visitor to be receptive to experiencing the performances that occur within."[1]

The largest of the venues is the Sosnoff Theater, a concert hall whose capacity was initially limited to 850 seats. It is hexagonal in plan, with orchestra stalls and two levels of balconies placed inside a concrete box completely lined with wood—a material that, according to Gehry, "psychologically enhances the feeling of music." He adds, "People relate to musical instruments that are made of wood, like the violins and the cellos. It doesn't have to be wood—wood is just the decoration—but it does have a psychological effect on people listening to music."[2] This wall treatment extends to the waves of the ceiling, a key element in the good acoustics of the room, calculated by Yasuhisa Toyota.

The vertical volume of the music hall sits in a steel cage, which is itself clad in steel. It is flanked by the Luma Theater, where the metal structure is left exposed, and by several dance and theater studios. The contrast between the restraint and austerity of the back part of the building and the fluid lyricism of the metal apron seems to echo Gehry's early processes and his projects from the 1990s, as if the Danziger Studio had mated with a cousin of the Bilbao museum. In a wooded landscape, celebrated by the painters of the Hudson River School, a skewed mirror is held up to nature.

The center's inauguration was the moment of truth. The size of the hall's orchestra pit had been calibrated for chamber operas, but the full depth of the hall itself could accommodate an entire opera in all its dimensions. The initial concert, however, was devoted to Gustav Mahler's Third Symphony. Gehry reported that "there were two passages where I thought my ears were going to split open, the pressure from the sound was so great,"[3] but adjustments to the shell conceived by Toyota canceled these unexpected effects.

1   Statement by Frank Gehry and Craig Webb, 2003.
2   Quoted in Barbara Isenberg, *Conversations with Frank Gehry* (New York: Alfred A. Knopf, 2009), 227.
3   Ibid., 229.

The lobby and the main stairs.

The Sosnoff Theater.

The façade on Vassar Street.

Ray and Maria Stata Center for MIT

Cambridge, Massachusetts, 1998–2004

General view looking northwest, with the MIT dome at left.

View of the ground-level interior street.

In the interior of Stata, we have a fairly open system and the people in the building can move stuff around and they don't have to call us. They don't have to feel that it's precious. It won't feel precious. It is simple and it's going to be simple in a couple of years. If anybody wants to move they can just go to the store, buy three sheets of plywood, and nail it up, finish it and they've got it. I think of this in terms of controlled chaos. I always relate it to democracy. Democracy is pluralism, the collision of ideas.

Frank Gehry, quoted in Nancy Joyce, *Building Stata: The Design and Construction of Frank O. Gehry's Stata Center* (Cambridge, MA: MIT Press, 2004), xi.

View of a robotics workshop.

Ray and Maria Stata Center for MIT
32 Vassar Street, Cambridge, Massachusetts, 1998–2004

In a break from the repeated slabs of laboratory buildings at the Massachusetts Institute of Technology (MIT), the center named after two of its principal donors, the computer science pioneer Ray Stata and his wife, gave Gehry a chance to pursue his work on the relationship between unity and diversity. The project illustrates a principle of differentiation through its vertical stratification, in which Gehry rewrites the familiar tripartite distinctions between base, mid-section, and crown in his own manner. The base of the building belongs to the ordering system of the campus. Inside, it enables the articulation of technical systems and the circulation of researchers connected to the labyrinthine spaces of MIT, whereas on the outside it provides usable spaces for students. While the building might superficially appear to be an arbitrary assemblage, the basement level of the center is in fact rooted in the many systems of the institution and helps unify them.

The initial idea was to bring together laboratories for computer science, artificial intelligence, and information and decision systems, along with the departments of linguistics and philosophy. Three main issues needed to be addressed: the provision of spaces for faculty, students, and support staff; the opening up of access to the eastern part of the campus; and the creation of places for social interaction.

After attempting to adhere to the orthogonal geometry of a massing plan laid out by Wallace Floyd in 1989, Gehry ultimately based the project around the best way of grouping the users, who had been consulted at length regarding their current usage and future aspirations for their workspaces. The program called for a "hierarchical organization that required spaces ranging in accessibility, from the totally open areas shared by members of a community to private offices for individual faculty members." In order to pin down an ideal grouping, Gehry proposed studying cultures far removed from the scientists he was interviewing and submitted proposals for a "Japanese house" with sliding screens, a loft-like space, a "prairie dog town," a "colonial manor," and a "village of orangutans"—which ended up being the final choice.

Once the laboratories, the robotics workshops, and the seminar rooms had been defined, they were grouped into what Gehry called "bottles," after those painted by Giorgio Morandi—a concept that took into account their height and verticality. As a result, "if you look at the connections between the parts—where each 'bottle' touches the next—it looks like one building, but there are ten. That's how we went about keeping it from seeming gargantuan and cold."[1]

The completed building is a landscape of volumes covered in brick, glass, and matte or shiny metal, that are bookended by two "towers," G and D, bearing the names of their respective donors, Bill Gates and Alexander W. Dreyfoos. The intense yellow of one of the "bottles" brings to mind Fernand Léger's painting of 1922, the *Femme allongée* (Reclining Woman). Contrasting with this dynamic spectacle, the public gallery on the ground floor unifies the building and makes it one of the most welcoming places in a campus infamous for its endless corridors.

---

1   Frank Gehry quoted in Nancy Joyce, *Building Stata: The Design and Construction of Frank O. Gehry's Stata Center* (Cambridge, MA: MIT Press, 2004), p. XI.

Detail of the exterior with the Dreyfoos tower at right.

View of the ground-level interior street.

The façade on Goebenstrasse.

MARTa

Herford, 1998–2005

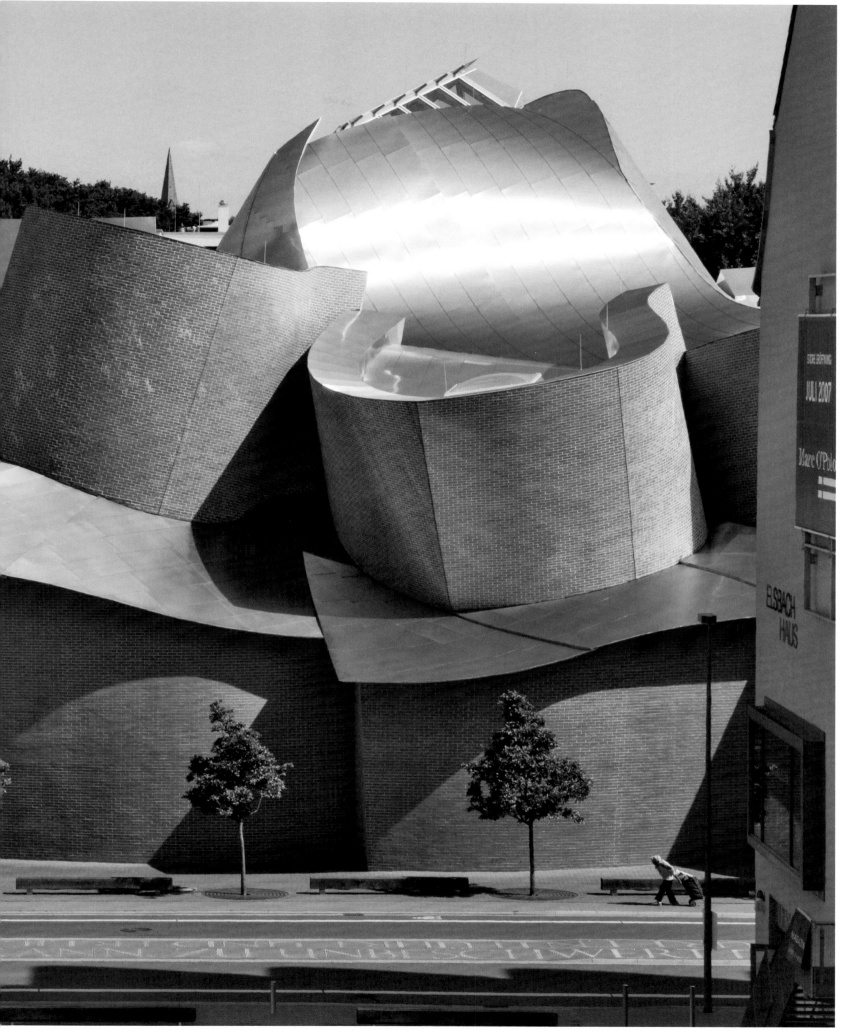

The main façade and the entrance.

View from the Aa river.

I've sat out on the back terrace of the museum already, overlooking the river, and it is all quite nice now.

Frank Gehry, quoted by Carly Berwick, *Metropolis*, vol. 24, no. 5 (May 2005), 34.

Wow! A pretty nice building. I was exploring the thin edge of the metal sheet—the knife edge. And I worked on the contrast between the brick and these surfaces.

Frank Gehry, interview with the author, Playa Vista, April 28, 2021.

MARTa
Goebenstrasse 2, Herford, 1998–2005

Set in a small city in Westphalia, this building serves as a showcase for the furniture and upholstery fabric industry, of which Herford has been a center for decades. First programmed in 1996, the institution positions itself at the crossroads of art and design. It aims at being more than a museum limited simply to conservation and display, and sets itself the goal of promoting interaction between professionals, artists, and the public. Its acronym refers to furniture (*Möbel* in German), art (in English), and environment (*ambiente* in Italian).

The new building is grafted, in a manner of speaking, onto the factory of the Ahlers clothing manufacturers, built in 1959 by the Wuppertal architect Walter Lippold. It hugs the factory and extends along two edges, one down the Goebenstrasse, and one overlooking the small river Aa. The project was conceived in close cooperation with Jan Hoet, who was named director of the institution at the outset of the project, and who managed in record time to assemble a collection representative of the directions taken by contemporary art.

Gehry's initial sketches and models defined orthogonal galleries, and he studied how they could best capture daylight in detail. He then moved some of them away from the existing building and developed a curvilinear device screening them off. Through numerous sketches over the course of the project's development, three distinct entities emerged. The first, a long volume, perpendicular to the street and pushed up against the building, would house the forum, an interactive space dedicated to public events. The second, separated from the first by the main entrance facing the city—and which ended up being relatively compact in the final built version—represents the core of MARTa. It resembles a sort of flower in plan, whose ovary is rectangular, and whose petals house the galleries. A restaurant—the Kupferbar, or Copper Bar—sits between this element and the bank of the Aa, to Gehry's obvious satisfaction.

Seen from the street, the existing building is concealed by a steel screen, perforated to spell out the name of the institution. This section contains the museum's main hall. The white reinforced-concrete walls are clad in a continuous surface of bricks that is stretched like a sort of mineral film and that extends above the level of the stainless-steel roof; occasional overhangs form canopies that reach down to the ground to enclose the restaurant.

Almost twenty years after his work on the Vitra museum, this time Gehry endeavored to respond to the materiality of the industrial architecture of northern Germany, whose vocabulary consists primarily of brick walls and steel coverings rather than white walls and zinc roofs.

The galleries are topped off with curvilinear ceilings and light wells, whose glazed areas are square in plan, echoing the mixture of geometries that is the true mark of a project subtly inserted in the existing fabric.

View of a gallery.

The Kupferbar.

Bird's-eye view looking east.

The pavilion with its background of high-rises.

Jay Pritzker Pavilion

Chicago, 1999–2004

Views of the stage during evening performances.

He said to me,
"You know, this is very Chicago."
And I said,
"I know, but I want it to be very Frank."

Cindy Pritzker, quoted in Paul Goldberger, *Building Art: The Life and Work of Frank Gehry* (New York: Alfred A. Knopf, 2015), 336.

The Pavilion is a highly sculptural design element clad in stainless steel panels. The stage area is clad in Douglas fir. The Pavilion is visible from surrounding city streets and is intended to act as a focal point for Millennium Park. The Pavilion features a series of portable risers that will accommodate an orchestra of up to 120 musicians, and a choral terrace with space for a choir of up to 150 members.... Large glass doors allow the Pavilion to be used during winter months for public functions including banquets, receptions, and lectures. A decorative lighting system enhances the Pavilion with colored light washes and projections during evening performances.

Office description, 2014. Gehry Partners.

Jay Pritzker Pavilion

201 E. Randolph Street, Chicago, 1999–2004

After the Columbian Exhibition of 1893, held to celebrate the rebirth of a city destroyed by fire twenty years earlier, the shoreline of Chicago along Lake Michigan was transformed according to the 1909 plan of Daniel H. Burnham. In the interwar period, the Art Institute grew toward the lake and crossed the railroad tracks of the Chicago Central line, but it was not until the end of the twentieth century that the tracks to the north of the museum were completely covered over by parkland, an extension of the park dedicated in 1901 to General Ulysses Grant. Reacting against the nostalgic design vocabulary supported by the then city mayor, Richard M. Daly, Cindy Pritzker—who with her husband, Jay, funded the world-renowned architecture prize named after them—exerted all her political influence in 1999 so that a project financed by her foundation would be commissioned from Gehry. At first, the municipality proposed that he simply produce a study for a façade to be inserted into the overall plan by Skidmore, Owings, and Merrill, which was meant to be completed by 2000. Subsequently, Gehry obtained the commission for a concert pavilion as well as additional design time, which enabled him to think it through in all its dimensions.

The pavilion complements the Petrillo Music Shell, built in Grant Park at the end of the 1970s. It is grafted onto the Harris Theater for Music and Dance, with which it shares rehearsal halls and backstage areas. It is meant to house music performances for four thousand listeners in fixed seating and an additional seven thousand sitting on a lawn that spreads over nearly 2.5 acres*.

Once again, Gehry's past experiences with open-air concert venues such as the Hollywood Bowl and the Columbia and Concord pavilions guided his thinking on the acoustic issues of the project. The parallel with the Hollywood Bowl is not just coincidental. Both projects must deal with a directional space, and the main issue is how to ensure that the sound is projected evenly across the full depth of the site. But unlike with the Los Angeles project, which featured ready-mades such as cardboard tubes and plastic spheres, by now Gehry had a language at his disposal that he had developed since the 1990s, and he possessed an unquestionable skill in deploying animated and expressive metal surfaces.

Here, the stage is covered by a sculptural assemblage of metal sheets. Gehry rejected the option of planting posts with speakers on top to broadcast the sound: "Then, as you sat on the lawn and listened to music, you'd be in a forest of posts. I felt that was not a good way to do it, and so I came up with the idea of a trellis in which the speakers were hung, so that the trellis formed a kind of sky. The trellis identified and created a sense of space, and the sound distribution works."[1] The waves of metal covering the stage were extended via a net over the expanse of the lawn. It was as if Louise Bourgeois's spider that sits in front of the Bilbao Guggenheim had come to spin her web on Lake Michigan.

*   1 ha.

1   Quoted in Barbara Isenberg, *Conversations with Frank Gehry* (New York: Alfred A. Knopf, 2009), 230.

Bird's-eye view of Millennium Park, showing the pavilion (center), Anish Kapoor's sculpture *Cloud Gate* (left), and Frank Gehry's BP pedestrian bridge (right).

The stage and the overhead trellis bearing speakers.

General view of the site from the ocean.

Biomuseo

Panama City, 2000–2014

The exterior stairs.

The reason that it is colorful is that Panama City is a Spanish colonial city, with red tiled roofs and white plaster walls.

Frank Gehry, quoted in an interview with Veronica Simpson, *Blueprint*, May 2014, 62.

This project was important for me because of Berta, and I wanted to do something special. But I have never been there to see the site. It looks great in the photos and it should work in the rain, which is the main challenge. In Panama, the rain can fall horizontally, with much wind. I am not sure how it works, but it seems to perform well.

Frank Gehry, interview with the author, Playa Vista, April 28, 2021.

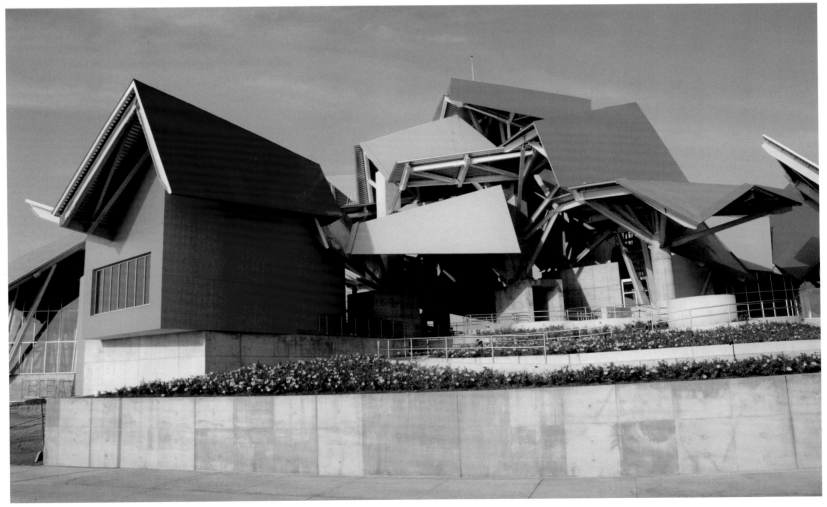

Partial view of the exterior.

The underside of the roof and its forest of pillars.

Biomuseo
Amador Causeway, Panama City, 2000–2014

Gehry had to wait almost forty years after his first projects in California to be finally invited to design a building in Latin America, despite the proximity of Los Angeles to Mexico and the south of the continent. His persistent involvement in this project owes as much to the Panamanian origins of Berta Aguilera, his wife since 1975, as to the seductive nature of the exceptional site. Even more than in Bilbao, and much like Jørn Utzon's opera house in the bay of Sydney, the project—a biodiversity museum— is considered in terms of its effect on the perception of the landscape from a distance. The site is located on the long peninsula of Amador, which projects into the Pacific Ocean at the entrance to the Panama Canal and serves in a way as an early signpost for it.

Since there were no buildings nearby, and the only visible context was the line of city skyscrapers on the horizon, the project was carried out with a certain freedom, the only constraint being the narrow dimensions of the spit of land on which it sits, previously occupied by an American military base. The plan is laid out in four directions around an open-air atrium in a manner more reminiscent of Bilbao than of Seattle.

Gehry made use of several analogies to define the main elements of the building. On the exterior, the intense colors of the metal roof plates, refined through lengthy studies in model form, evoke the feathers of the guacamaya parrot, the bird that serves as the symbol of the region. With their vertical supports, the tree-like pieces of steel and occasional openings allow daylight to filter through, and the galleries evoke the protective canopies of tropical forests.

Concrete stairs connect the forecourt to the elevated atrium, whose topmost point reaches 30 m* in height and is accessible to visitors at no charge. At the upper level, a café covered by a rainbow-colored roof recalls the curve of the Bridge of the Americas, spanning the entrance to the canal. Under this public area and benefiting from bright, open views toward the bay is an open-air gallery devoted to the "Human Path." It leads to a series of thematic galleries, each one of which has a unique form, that address both the ecology and the history of Panama: there is a "Gallery of Biodiversity"; one dedicated to the "Living Web"; a presentation of the relations between the two Americas, entitled "Worlds Collide"; and another on the relationship between the Atlantic and the Pacific, entitled "Oceans Divided." The narrative is anchored in its local context through the "Panarama," a gallery named "Building the Bridge," and an exploration of the area with the slogan, "It's Panama that is the museum." These eight galleries were conceived by the visionary designer Bruce Mau, who, like Gehry, was originally from Ontario, and whose role in the interior disposition established certain limits to the architectural design. Unlike the art museums in which his affinity with the works presented leads him to shape galleries responding to their forms and textures, here Gehry had to settle for creating the best possible conditions for the unfolding of a spectacular and didactic narrative.

* 98 ft.

Partial view of the exterior.

Neighboring houses reflected on the Dundas Street façade.

Art Gallery of Ontario

Toronto, 2000–2008

The main façade on Dundas Street.

View of the atrium along the main axis of the museum.

I was more interested in making the street a commercial project, a normal street, with shops alongside it. The entrance before was terrible, much worse than the one I remembered from my childhood. We reorganized the entire museum so you came in at the center, in the axis of the historic building in the center. I was excited to include the little houses across the road as the view. That's why I made the long gallery above the stairs, which they've never used properly. I had arranged a great John Chamberlain show, with sixty pieces, and the director nixed it. It would have given it its true meaning.

Frank Gehry, interview with the author, Playa Vista, April 28, 2021.

The contemporary art wing, seen from the south.

Art Gallery of Ontario
317 Dundas Street West, Toronto, 2000–2008

The commission for an extension to Canada's premier art museum—the Art Gallery of Ontario, or AGO—allowed Gehry to retrace the footsteps of his youth, as the museum is close to the house his grandparents lived in, at 15 Beverly Street, and because he himself had frequented the gallery as a child with his mother. The museum was founded in 1900 in the central neighborhood of Grange Park and had never stopped growing through the acquisition of small buildings and the construction of annexes. The museum was cruelly deficient in clarity as to its circulation paths and its presence in the city at the scale of urban space. Its plan, which centered on the Walker Court, a large, columned hall built in 1935 by the office of Darling and Pearson, had become illegible owing to the addition of an entrance at the northeast corner of the site during the 1970s. A rewriting of the ensemble was called for, as well as new facilities suitable for receiving the public and for the display of contemporary art.

The donation of a collection of two thousand artworks, along with a significant amount of money, by the prosperous businessman and collector Ken Thompson enabled the AGO to embark on a comprehensive building program. In keeping with the empathetic attitude that Gehry generally shows toward existing buildings, he made every effort to study and to understand the character of each space before intervening to complete it, redesign it, or modify its role in the sequence of the museum visit.

The entrance on Dundas Street, at the center of the museum that Gehry had known in his childhood, was returned to its former preeminence. It marks the beginning of an axial sequence (interrupted at one point by a spiral ramp for handicapped visitors, treated like a sinuous wood sculpture) and leads through the Walker Court to the quaint Grange House, a witness to the beginnings of the museum. The entrance is located in the middle of a glazed hall, with doors opening onto the street, and is encased within a curved, glazed structure that extends the full length of the building. This glass tube, which one might compare to a Native-American canoe laid on its side, becomes the main urban component of the institution, especially after nightfall, when it casts a warm light onto Dundas Street, one of the principal east–west arteries of Toronto. Its concave glue-laminated wood structure is left exposed on the interior, marking the rhythm of the long sculpture gallery on the floor above.

On the south side of the museum, the large volume of the galleries intended for contemporary art is clad in blue titanium. A helical stair in gray metal emerges from the exterior façade, a counterpart to the one finished in Douglas fir created inside the Walker Court, where it provides a link between its upper level and the new galleries and completes the varied palette of materials and finishes deployed in the new spaces. At the lower level, Gehry has designed undulating vitrines, like vertical waves of glass, to house Ken Thompson's collection of ship models.

The glazed gallery running along Dundas Street.

The undulating rooftop as seen above a vineyard.

Marqués de Riscal Hotel

Eltziego, 2003–6

General view with the church of San Andrés.

Detail of the titanium-clad roof envelope.

I spend a lot of time selecting the materials, the details, and the way a project is going to be built: the expression. It's about the feeling, the perception of the building as a sensibility. If you want to be involved with the visual world and make things that are visual, then you have to look at everything. I spend all my time looking at things and learning about them. There was a period when I used to look into my wastepaper basket and fantasize buildings and forms.

Frank Gehry, quoted in Mark Rappolt and Robert Violette (eds.), *Gehry Draws* (Cambridge, MA: MIT Press/Violette Editions, 2004), 250.

View of the envelope.

Marqués de Riscal Hotel
Torrea Kalea 1, Eltziego, 2003–6

Above the vineyards of La Rioja, whose grapes produce a red wine with an established international reputation, floats a large titanium flower. It seems to be an outcrop in the landscape of the *terroir* but is in fact an observatory offering a vast panorama of vine stock laid out in rows as far as the eye can see, covering 1,400 ha.* in the Sierra Cantabria. The Marqués de Riscal winery, whose products are distributed across five continents, decided to create a "City of Wine" in the heart of the Basque countryside and judged it necessary to have a center and architectural signpost.

The small town of Eltziego found itself fitted out with tourist facilities, chief among which was a luxury hotel connected to the producers' wine cellars and commissioned from Frank Gehry. The polychrome waves of the roof derive from those of the Biomuseo in Panama City, as if the planar surfaces of the latter had been replaced by undulating ones.

The contrast they form with the deliberately orthogonal volumes of the lower parts of the building, and the superposition of two different geometries, produce the sort of duality that is at work in the vertical direction in the Richard B. Fisher Center. Gehry's working method is more clearly evident here than in most of his other projects from the early 2000s. It consists of setting out an arrangement of cubic volumes, evaluating its practical qualities and internal relations, and enveloping it in a metal superstructure that is both fragmented and porous.

A large underground cellar, invisible from the outside, was excavated, and the building was placed on top; a glass elevator provides access to the cellar. Three service levels for the hotel are located above ground. The first two levels are housed in rectilinear volumes clad in the beige sandstone used in the houses of the nearby village of Eltziego, as well as in its sixteenth-century church of San Andrés. The hotel reception, on the ground floor, allows access to the rooms. Gehry designed them in full, including the double-curved maple headboards. The restaurant on the top level affords a view of the landscape framed by the lower edges of the roofing. Other rooms, added late in the project by the chosen management, are linked to the building via a metal footbridge.

The reinforced-concrete structure extends upward in a network of V-shaped posts that support the roof grid, which is finished off with leaves of titanium and steel. The equally complex and changing curvature of these surfaces, which were composed in vertical waves in the initial sketches, is colored in a manner that refers back to the materiality of wine production, which the hotel offers up as spectacle. The purple tint of the titanium recalls the dark hue of the Rioja wine, and the reflective silver of the metal sheets echoes the foil wrapped around the corks. Finally, the net in which bottles by Marqués de Riscal are usually sold is the origin behind the gold tint on the titanium leaves slipped in between the undulating surfaces.

*   3,500 acres

View of a hotel terrace.

View of the stone-faced façade from the village.

View of the tower's summit.

8 Spruce Street Apartment Tower

New York, 2003–11

The tower against the Manhattan skyline as viewed from Brooklyn.

Interior view of an apartment with the Woolworth Building and the New York Bay.

I used to stay at the Four Seasons Hotel when I was in New York and just after we got the Beekman project, I was there for meetings.... I asked for a room on a high floor so I could look at the buildings. I just stared out the window at them, trying to understand the typology of New York City a little better. I also walked around the city a lot and looked at the buildings from street level and came to conclusions that were used to build Beekman. I think that's why Beekman has that look.

Frank Gehry, quoted in Barbara Isenberg, *Conversations with Frank Gehry* (New York: Alfred A. Knopf, 2009), 225.

8 Spruce Street Apartment Tower

8 Spruce Street, New York, 2003–11

This is not only the first tower that Gehry ever built, but it also marks the beginning of a new cycle in New York architecture, becoming the highest residential building in a city that has since seen a proliferation of even higher examples—towers whose profiles have been compared to pins or pencils.

Gehry's first opportunity to design a Manhattan skyscraper was in 1987, on the occasion of a competition held for the site of Madison Square Garden on which he collaborated with David Childs, of Skidmore, Owings, and Merrill, who familiarized him with the arcana of this building type. With Childs and the developer Bruce Ratner, Gehry participated in the 2000 competition for the New York Times Building on Eighth Avenue, working on the public spaces and in particular the crown at its summit that evoked a flame. Renzo Piano would be awarded the commission, while Ratner asked Gehry to work on a delicate undertaking: a development for the railroad tracks at the Atlantic Yards in Brooklyn, which would be abandoned a few years later. In the meantime, the apartment building located near New York City Hall, between Beekman and Spruce Streets, had started construction.

Innumerable variants of the tower were considered, notably in models that used every material imaginable and explored multiple modes of twisting its volumes in order to find a sculptural language that could stand up to the most remarkable skyscrapers in Manhattan and mark a complete contrast to the most trivial ones. A confrontation with the nearby Woolworth Building and its successive setback profile was unavoidable, which led to the development of three volumes, decreasing in width, in a T-shaped plan.

The base of the tower is a blocky volume clad in brick, which contains six stories of a city elementary school and one level of medical facilities. The seventy-six-story tower sits on top of it, having nearly lost twenty floors during the financial crisis of 2008. The façade of the apartment tower is practically flat on the south side. It is oriented toward Wall Street, so as to conform to the norms of typical residential units in New York, over which Gehry had no control. The other three sides, with their sinuous lines, are radically different from the orthogonal base. They are expressions of a sculptural approach that Gehry has linked back to his admiration for the folds created by the Roman sculptor Gianlorenzo Bernini, which the art historian Irving Lavin had pointed out to him, and whose angular qualities he prefers to the more fluid lines of the work of Michelangelo, which captivate him nonetheless.[1]

There are two hundred different apartment plans, all containing essentially orthogonal rooms where only the exterior wall is curved to follow the lines of the façade. The latter consists of ten thousand steel panels produced in Japan, and each panel required a unique design. By virtue of the tight angles, some rooms have lateral views into the neighboring apartments, which frame more distant perspectives as well. The three levels of collective services, which include a swimming pool, establish a certain continuity between this building and the vertical apartment hotels of the early twentieth century.

1   Jackie Cooperman, "Frank Gehry: A sit-down with the artist of architecture," *Wall Street Journal*, April 2, 2011.

The tower with the Woolworth Building and the South Street Seaport.

The sinuous folds on the façade.

General view from Washington Avenue.

New World Center

Miami Beach, 2003–11

Evening view from Washington Avenue, showing the landscaping by West 8.

A crevice between two interior volumes.

You just need to have a space where you can really do this, and I just see the whole thing. I really would need to build this building for you.... In terms of our relationship, the more you tell me what you want and what you like and what you don't like, the better the building will be that you get. You have to really tell me.

Frank Gehry, quoted in Paul Goldberger, *Building Art: The Life and Work of Frank Gehry* (New York: Alfred A. Knopf, 2015), 405.

New World Center
500 17th Street, Miami Beach, 2003–11

Ever since his initial projects for concert pavilions, Frank Gehry has not only worked closely with acoustic engineers such as Christopher Jaffe or Yasuhisa Toyota, but has also established long-lasting relationships with directors of musical venues such as Ernest Fleischmann and conductors including Esa-Pekka Salonen, in both cases in Los Angeles. But his bond with Michael Tilson Thomas is an exceptional one: they have known each other since the conductor was a child, and Gehry was his babysitter during California summers spent in Idyllwild. Gehry had been struck at the time by his precocious musical talents.

Thomas became a musical director after training with Leonard Bernstein and working for the Los Angeles Philharmonic. He created the New World Symphony in Miami, a teaching program to prepare musicians for concert symphonies. After meeting Gehry at the Aspen Music Festival in 2002, he commissioned a new building from him. Shortly thereafter, the municipality of Miami Beach proposed a rectangular plot in the south of the city, three blocks from the Atlantic Ocean.

The siting of the building can be compared to that of the Centre Pompidou in Paris, with its rectangular footprint and its volume facing an esplanade— a mineral space in the case of the Paris museum, and a heavily planted one here. But the comparison stops there. Gehry's first sketches show a tentacular form spreading out from the center of the block, accessible from Lincoln Avenue via a sort of passageway.

Thomas was fairly set in his expectations for the architecture. He invoked Kurt Schwitters's *Merzbau* as a possible source. He was also inspired by the projects by Gehry with which he was already acquainted, which led him initially to propose an ensemble of autonomous volumes of increasing sizes, ranging from the smallest chambers to the concert hall proper, and to imagine them as so many forms that could be enclosed within a large glass container.

As built, the project retains the idea of transparency toward urban space, but the glass outer skin is limited to the east façade of an apparently conventional rectangular volume. Rather than adding clustered elements, as he had done in many of his projects since the Vitra museum, Gehry proposed to deploy the complex forms with which he might be associated within a sort of strait-jacket, saying that "We'll put the juice on the inside."[1]

The orthogonal matrix of the glass façade is visible from Washington Avenue through the undulating lines of palm trees that defined the park, which was designed by the Dutch landscape architects West 8 and given a soundscape audible to passers-by. It is possible to make out the white volumes inside the hall tumbling down, and the main staircase weaving through. The seats in the concert hall are arranged according to the "vineyard principle" employed by Hans Scharoun in the Berlin Philharmonie, with seating all around the stage. At only one-third the size of the Los Angeles concert hall, the inside space is extended thanks to large suspended screens onto which images are projected during performances. This play between sound and image is amplified outside, where the great wall of the concert hall becomes a giant screen after nightfall, enabling the whole city to participate in the programs inside the center.

1   Quoted in Paul Goldberger, *Building Art: The Life and Work of Frank Gehry* (New York: Alfred A. Knopf, 2015), 406.

The auditorium during a performance.

General view from the east, with the reflecting pool.

Louis Vuitton Foundation

Paris, 2004–14

The lecture theater, with works by Ellsworth Kelly.

Aerial view looking east, with Paris in the distance.

Detail of the envelope.

Lou Ruvo Center for Brain Health

Las Vegas, 2005–10

General view.

The open space between the center and the Cleveland Clinic.

Before Larry Ruvo called me, I turned down every project that came to me for Las Vegas.... It's not that I am against gambling. My father sold slot machines. Pinball machines. It was the carny business, and I grew up in that, so I wasn't judgmental. But the few times I had been to Vegas, I'd seen all those people, like lemmings, putting money in. I think it's a substitute for sex for those people. It seemed so negative that I just didn't want to be part of it. I couldn't imagine designing a place that would contribute to those needs. When I design a building, I want to feel like I'm contributing something.

Frank Gehry, quoted in Barbara Isenberg, *Conversations with Frank Gehry* (New York: Alfred A. Knopf, 2009), 234.

Lou Ruvo Center for Brain Health

888 W. Bonneville Avenue, Las Vegas, 2005–10

In order for Gehry to overcome his professed loathing for Las Vegas, whose elevation to the canon in Robert Venturi and Denise Scott Brown's memorable book of 1972[1] had done little to blunt, he had to meet a client who was on the same wavelength. This happened to be the liquor and wine merchant Larry Ruvo, a socialite who wanted to celebrate the memory of his father, Lou, who had succumbed in 1994 to Alzheimer's. Ruvo proposed to build a branch of the Cleveland Clinic, the leading hospital in Ohio, to specialize in research on this disease. Gehry was won over by Ruvo and accepted the challenge, on the condition that the center also include a laboratory devoted to the study of Huntington's disease, which his psychoanalyst, Milton Wexler, was battling at the time.

In the Symphony Park area—located between the center of the city and Interstate 15, the highway that leads to Los Angeles, and the neighborhood where Las Vegas is attempting to establish a cultural identity—Gehry felt free to ignore the vulgarity of the Strip and its casinos, and imagine a form that to some extent evoked the convolutions of the human brain. In the 1970s his architecture had liberated itself from slavish servitude to wooden frames. His buildings from the beginning of the new millennium, such as this one, are distanced from his previous projects on account of their façades, which look as if they are in revolt. Drawing on several projects where the cladding had freed itself from the structure, the solution adopted here, after extensive research in model form, succeeded in linking the fairly static building unit of the Cleveland Clinic, masked by an undulating metal surface, with the center itself, which appears at first glance to be a pile of blocks fallen from the sky that bumped into each other during their fall.

The ensemble is more than a single building, recalling the image of a brain and its hemispheres. It is divided both horizontally, with the hospital block overlooking the asphalt expanse of a parking lot and the center facing the avenue, and vertically, where the prismatic volumes of the lower level are in a sense engulfed by a play of cubic forms with curvilinear edges. These are pierced by a grid of rectangular windows that transform the surfaces into lattices. An open space separates the two buildings, covered by the overhanging façades that provide some shade but are most likely incapable of providing sufficient protection from the desert sun.

The image of fragmentation visible on the exterior is deceiving, for these cubes have only five sides and are a long way from marking individual, distinct spaces. In fact, on the inside they correspond to a heterogeneous arrangement of the main circulation elements, the large lecture hall with its 450 seats, the library, and the other public spaces. They generate a changing play of light and shadow, lending ambiguity to the view one has when one looks up, similar to the way Giambattista Piranesi handled projections of height and depth in his imagined prison interiors. Although the surfaces here are white, the perspectives remain indecipherable, as in an etching by M. C. Escher.

1   Robert Venturi, Denise Scott Brown, and Steven Izenour, *Learning from Las Vegas* (Cambridge, MA: MIT Press, 1972).

Worm's-eye view of the ceiling.

Aerial view of the UTS campus.

Dr. Chau Chak Wing Building, UTS

Ultimo, New South Wales, 2009–14

Detail of the brick façade.

Interior view of the reinforced-concrete structure.

The stairs linking the two lower levels.

A trunk and core of activity and branches for people to connect and do their private work.

Frank Gehry, quoted by Sebastian Jordana, *Archdaily*, December 23, 2010.

Maybe it's a brown paper bag, but it's flexible on the inside, there's a lot of room for changes or movement.

Jonathan Pearlman, "Frank Gehry unveils 'squashed brown paper bag' building in Sydney," *Telegraph*, February 3, 2015.

Dr. Chau Chak Wing Building, UTS

14–28 Ultimo Road, Ultimo, New South Wales, 2009–14

The University of Technology Sydney (UTS) is located in the city's former industrial quarter of Haymarket, where certain buildings from that period and the earlier urban structure still remain. It can be found at the end of a "cultural ribbon" that starts with none other than Jørn Utzon's opera house. The plot occupied by the business school, named after its principal donor, the Chinese businessman Chau Chak Wing, is situated on Ultimo Road, below the Omnibus Line and bordering on the Goods Line, two abandoned railway tracks that have become the main pedestrian axes for the campus.

Like the Ray and Maria Stata Center at MIT, the building is divided vertically into open spaces for the public on the lower floors, and seminar rooms, offices, and more private spaces on the upper floors. In this way, the building contributes to the policy of pooling resources between buildings and opening up the campus to the city.

The visual relationship with its immediate context is particularly well developed. On the Omnibus Line, the building seems twice the size, its lower floors appearing to extend the lines of the old factories, while the divided upper part serves as a signal. On the other hand, the great glazed area of the façade is continuous and reflects adjacent buildings on its angled surfaces.

This seemingly fortress-like building can be entered from several sides. The upper entrance on the Omnibus Line is actually at the same level as the second floor of the building. It leads down to the ground floor via a staircase draped in stainless steel. On the inside, the reinforced-concrete structure is exposed, with large diagonal members crossing the central volume, from which the layout of the teaching facilities for the school's highly personalized curriculum is also visible. Their placement and their lighting were studied via large models registering the precise location of every table and every chair. Each space is treated in a specific manner, the most remarkable being the seminar room on the ground floor, which is a kind of shed made of thick blocks of wood for soundproofing that resemble those used in the house on Adelaide Drive (see Frank and Berta Gehry House, pp. 348–59).

But it was the design and construction of its outer skin that made this building yet another step forward for the Gehry office. The characteristic undulations of the façade, which does not include one single straight line (except for the window frames and glazing), were made possible by the systematic use of three hundred and twenty thousand bricks specially designed using CATIA software. Five different models of brick were employed, which could respond to every situation, create relief effects, and generate a masterly play of shadows. The shape of the bricks, manufactured by the Bowral factory in the Indian Punjab, is sometimes contoured, as with the Model K brick, which includes an angular projection. Unlike the metal façades of Gehry's buildings, which since 1990 have generally been fabricated by specialized companies such as Permasteelisa, an Italian firm that has since gone global, the construction of this building was carried out by specialized tradesmen under the leadership of the master brickmason Peter Favetti, who explicitly saw their work on this project as the revalorization of a trade dismissed as obsolete.

View of the interior from above, with the lecture hall on the left.

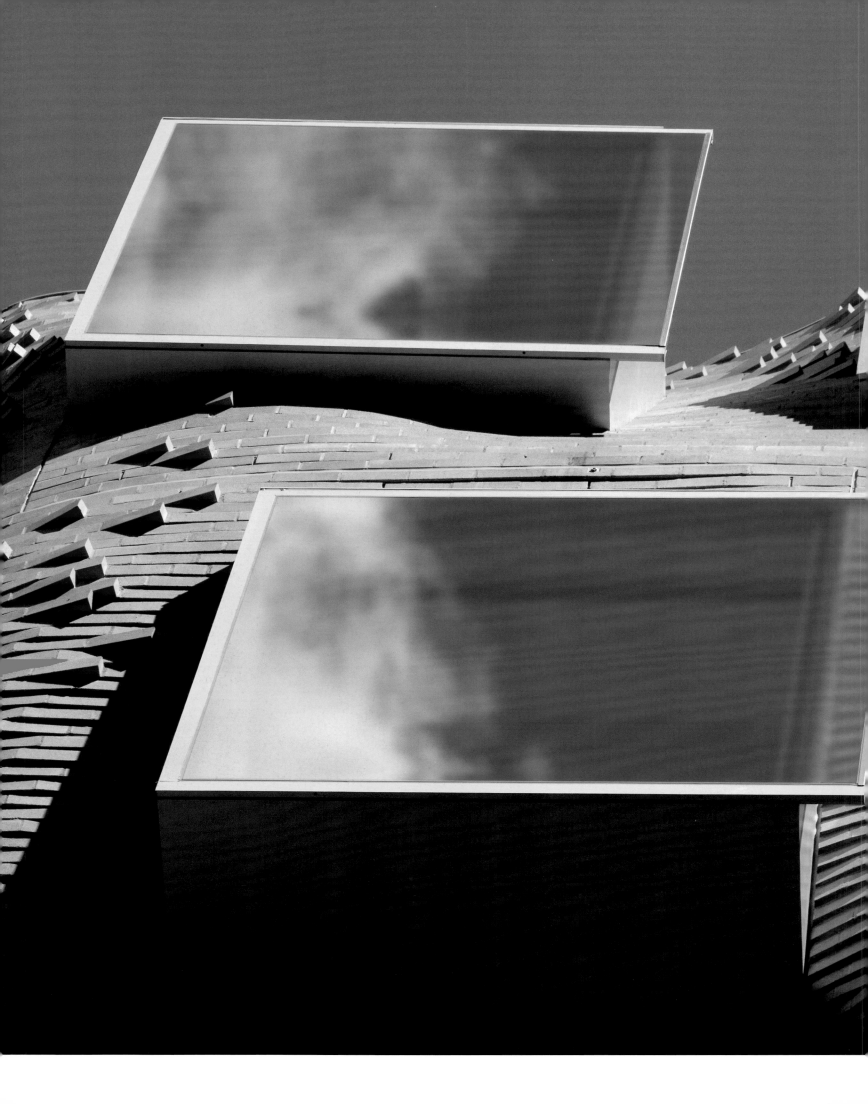

Detail of the brick cladding.

WE LOOK UPON THIS SHAKEN EART[H]

THE BUILDING OF A PEACE WITH JUSTICE IN A WO[RLD]

SECOND INAUGURAL ADDRESS · JANUARY 21, 1957

Corner view with the Capitol in the background.

Dwight D. Eisenhower Memorial

Washington, DC, 2009–20

The memorial and the Department of Education visible through the steel mesh.

BECAUSE NO MAN IS REALLY A MAN WHO HAS LOST
WANT TO SPEAK FIRST OF THE DREAMS OF A
BE OF A STREET CAR CONDUCTOR OR HE SEES HIMSELF
ALL HE MAY REACH TO A POSITION OF LOCOMOTIVE
IS THAT DAY WHEN HE FINALLY COMES HOME. COMES
HOME TOWN. BECAUSE TODAY THAT DREAM OF MINE OF
REALIZED BEYOND THE WILDEST STRETCHES OF MY OWN
TO THANK YOU. TO SAY THE PROUDEST THING I CAN
HOMECOMING SPEECH, ABILENE,

Dwight D. Eisenhower as a young man: a sculpture by Sergey Eylanbekov.

I came away blindsided. It brings tears to my eyes.
How his accomplishments as a general and as a president
match anything, all without the fanfare that's going on
around the president now. The opposite. He was modest
but strong. A staggering accomplishment.

Frank Gehry on Eisenhower, in Rowan More, "Frank Gehry on his Memorial to Eisenhower," *Guardian*, September 6, 2020.

Dwight D. Eisenhower Memorial
540 Independence Avenue SW, Washington, DC, 2009–20

Aside from an unbuilt design for an extension to the Corcoran Gallery in 1998, Gehry had never had an opportunity to work in Washington before he won the competition, over forty-three other architects, for the construction of a monument to Dwight D. Eisenhower. The general served two terms as president of the United States after commanding the Allied Forces in Europe during World War II. But it took more than ten years of public controversy before the monument was finally inaugurated, in September 2020.

On a 4-acre* site along Constitution Avenue, between the massive volumes of the National Air and Space Museum and the Department of Education, Gehry proposed to build a park, with the monument serving as a screen to mask the ugliness of the latter. This steel tapestry in three pieces was intended to be accompanied by a group of sculptures, but these became a flash point for scandal. The theater director Robert Wilson had suggested to Gehry that he look to the hero's childhood for inspiration. He referred to the speech that the victorious Eisenhower had given in his birthplace of Abilene, Kansas: "Because no man is really a man who has lost out of himself all of the boy, I want to speak first of the dreams of a barefoot boy."

Gehry considered that Eisenhower's "modesty was his strength. He knew what he wanted, and he was as tough as nails,"[1] and he adopted this program, suggesting that a sculpture of the future general as a child be placed in the center of the composition, with an image of a Kansas landscape on a screen behind him. This concept was approved by the general's grandson, but it was vehemently opposed by his sisters, Ann and Susan, by the general's son, John, and by the National Civic Art Society and its president, Justin Shubow—a fanatical proponent of classical architecture and particularly ill disposed toward Gehry. Shubow would achieve his goal in 2020 by inspiring Donald Trump to issue a directive prescribing the classical style for all federal buildings. Innumerable meetings were organized while the press continued to make the most of the affair, until the project was approved in 2015. Although it was reduced in scale to just one panel, the Obama presidency finally released funds for its construction.

The solution that was ultimately adopted retains a screen 447 ft.[†] long, held up by seven pillars 80 ft.[‡] high that are clad in Spanish Ambar sandstone, while a statue of the young Ike, by Sergey Eylanbekov, has found a place in the corner of the square. The idea of reproducing a photograph using a braid of steel mesh was inspired by tapestries created by the hyperrealist painter Chuck Close based on his paintings. With the approval of the Eisenhower family, the theme of the Kansas countryside was replaced by a dramatic aerial view of the Pointe du Hoc—where furious combat took place at dawn on D-Day, June 6, 1944—showing a large expanse of wooded Normandy countryside with menacing clouds above. This realistic subject mirrors the discreet inscription that Gehry had woven onto the garage at Santa Monica Place in 1978 and testify to the freedom of visual expression that the architect has achieved over the years.

* 1.6 ha.
† 136 m
‡ 24 m

1 Quoted in Paul Goldberger, *Building Art: The Life and Work of Frank Gehry* (New York: Alfred A. Knopf, 2015), 413.

Bird's-eye view of the memorial and the gardens.

The memorial and the gardens on Constitution Avenue.

View of a sitting area on the upper level.

Frank and Berta Gehry House

Santa Monica, 2010–18

The house and garden as seen from Adelaide Drive.

View of the main living room.

Sam is easier to work with than I am. I did nothing, except plan with Berta how we would use the house.

Frank Gehry, quoted by Victoria Newhouse, "Exclusive Look Inside Frank Gehry's Home," *Architectural Record*, June 2019.

I can tell you now, at the end of the day, that each one of these rooms is spectacular. The living room is spectacular. That little room in the den is beautiful. This is all Sam, who knew about my wood thing at the Serpentine Gallery, which he had taken up and finished when I was with my daughter Leslie, who was dying. It was a moment of truth. He took over and he did it well. I think my main interference was in the front yard, where I put the trees and the planters and stuff like that in between, and the stuff that's not so good.

Frank Gehry, interview with the author, Playa Vista, April 28, 2021.

Frank and Berta Gehry House
Adelaide Drive, Santa Monica, 2010–18

Over the years, the house that Frank Gehry built for his family in 1978 had become too small and too inconvenient, despite the successive transformations and additions, which had left him rather unconvinced. As he himself would admit, "Once I touched it, the whole thing began to unravel. It got tarted up." He realized he was blocked: "I was emotionally trapped because it was this icon."[1] In order to break the spell, he decided to build a new house for his wife and himself, as the children were living independently. Gehry produced numerous studies for a first version, for a flat site in Venice, near Lincoln Boulevard. His way of cutting up the house into pavilions was retained in the final project, designed several years later in a collaboration between Gehry and his son Sam.

Adelaide Drive, the roadway the house is situated on, overlooks Santa Monica Canyon like a corniche. It is where the writer Christopher Isherwood lived for thirty years, and features remarkable bungalows from the beginning of the twentieth century. Aside from the view to the Pacific, on the horizon, from the site one can make out a grove of eucalyptus trees that conceals the house of Charles and Ray Eames, to which I had compared Gehry's house in the early 1980s.[2]

Pulled back and slightly elevated from the street, the new residence is oriented to the west and extends deep into the site. The main part is laid out in a butterfly plan, with two projecting wings whose roofs are glazed and supported by solid beams of Douglas fir that serve to frame the building. Unlike the lighter structures in Gehry's early construction—thin sections that he employed for architectural effect by exposing them—these elements, used in other projects such as the pavilion of the Serpentine Gallery in 2008 but rarely as systematically, have an undeniably structuring presence.

Opening onto a front garden that highlights the view toward the ocean, the two ground-floor wings make up the most public part of the house. The master bedroom takes up a generous amount of space on the upper level. Behind this core, a long pool and a gallery covered by a pergola stretch out in parallel through a garden that leads to a second building with a more tranquil and rectangular plan. It contains guest rooms, a sports room, and, most importantly, a room for chamber music, where Daniel Barenboim, among others, has given concerts on occasion. Designed to be completely energy-neutral, this little domestic village is equipped with sophisticated technical systems conceived by Transsolar, a consulting firm in Stuttgart specializing in the most advanced projects.

As for the building's structural features, compared with the apparent fragility of the house from 1978, the sturdy construction of the complex serves as an eloquent metaphor for the recognition that Gehry has finally come to enjoy in Los Angeles.

1   Nicolai Ouroussoff, "Mr. Gehry Builds His Dream House," *The New York Times*, January 9, 2005.
2   Jean-Louis Cohen, "Charles Eames, Frank O. Gehry: la maison manifeste," *Architecture, mouvement, continuité*, vol. 15, nos. 54–55 (July–September 1981), 77–85.

The balcony overlooking the ground floor.

The ground-floor den.

The music room at the end of the garden.

The house and the lap pool viewed from the music room.

The façade on Französische Strasse.

Pierre Boulez Saal

Berlin, 2011–17

The hall seen from the balcony.

The orchestra has to feel the audience, the audience has to feel the orchestra. When they do that, the orchestra plays better, and the audience hears better.... They're going to be more intimately connected to the music. I remember concerts in LA, people walked out on Boulez. I think this could invite you in more intimately than in a bigger hall.

Frank Gehry, in Joshua Barone, "Frank Gehry and Daniel Barenboim on Their New Concert Hall in Berlin," *The New York Times*, March 3, 2017.

The hall and the balcony, seen from the ground floor.

Pierre Boulez Saal
Französische Strasse 33D, Berlin, 2011–17

For decades, Gehry maintained strong ties with many notable musicians. The concert hall built for the Israeli–Argentinian conductor and pianist Daniel Barenboim, located in the historic center of what was formerly Prussian Berlin, is dedicated to Pierre Boulez, whom Gehry had known since his legendary "rug concerts" in the New York Lincoln Center in 1973. He and the architect had engaged in intense correspondence during the development of the Walt Disney Concert Hall.

In 1999 Barenboim created the Wedo, or West–Eastern Divan Orchestra, alongside the writer and university professor Edward Said. Every summer, the Wedo brought together young musicians from Israel, Palestine, and several Arab countries. To house the rehearsals and the concerts of the Barenboim-Said Akademie, Barenboim was assigned the premises previously used to store the sets of the State Opera of East Berlin. The hall is unnoticeable from the street and is nestled inside a stuccoed brick building, tidily located at the corner of two streets.

There is clearly a comparison to be made with the conference hall of the DZ Bank, located a few blocks away on the Pariser Platz. But here the ambitions—and the budgets—were much more modest. The initial sketches highlighted their similarity, showing a curvilinear form contained within an orthogonal container. Unlike the bank, the load-bearing walls of this particular container—a hall seating 682—were a constraint.

A hall, with an escalator passing through it from top to bottom, separates the classrooms of the Akademie, set up in the former offices of the Opera, from the concert space, where a sketch dedicated to Pierre Boulez describes the adopted design approach. It shows a spiral whose exterior outline is an oval, but which has a circular central void. An amusing neologism refers to it as "ovalable," that is to say, both oval and adjustable. As Irving Lavin maliciously pointed out to Gehry, the oval fits perfectly over the one in the floor plan of San Carlo alle Quattro Fontane, the small church built in Rome in 1646 by Francesco Borromini. But the form takes on a very different meaning in Berlin, where the oval is placed diagonally inside a rectangle, and the plan is not oriented toward an altar but centered on the orchestra. The tiers can be moved, or even made to partially disappear, in order to modify the configuration of the musicians.

At the second level, a cantilevered balcony, fixed in place and finished in wood like the seats at the lower floor, undulates between the four walls of the former warehouse like the track of a velodrome. It affords the two rows of spectators views over the soloists and orchestra, or sometimes even views of musicians placed at the same level as them, a level prescribed by Yasuhisa Toyota higher than Gehry would have liked. In a material reminder of the project's link to California, continuous paneling in Douglas fir contributes to the subtle acoustics of the hall while allowing the building's grid of rectangular windows to appear. Among the hall's many possible configurations, it would it seem perfectly possible to open up the lower floor completely and, once the seats have been put away, to recreate that intimate relationship with music that was a feature of the "rug concerts" in an authentic homage to Boulez.

The hall, with the musician's platform.

The foundation as seen from the Roman amphitheater.

Luma Foundation

Arles, 2007–21

Bird's-eye view with the Parc des Ateliers.

The tower at night.

Maja showed me around the city and described her feelings. She asked me to make a painterly building, with views over the campus and the town from various levels. There is a magnificent Roman amphitheater in the town, and Roman planned cities are something I have studied and I'm certainly inspired by them, but not literally. The idea of having the drum as a public space on boulevard Victor Hugo, this seemed like a perfect way to create a public center for the building. Maja wanted it to be open to the public and to create a place that would be used. As you go up in the spaces, they are more private and then at the top you have a view over the city. There was a time when this city was inside the Roman amphitheater. In some ways, we are building a drum with the city of Luma inside.

Frank Gehry, quoted in an interview with Veronica Simpson, *Blueprint*, May 2014, 62.

The tower of the town hall (left), the bell tower of Saint-Trophime (center), and the foundation (right).

Luma Foundation

33 avenue Victor-Hugo, Arles, 2007–21

Located near the Mediterranean, the project for the Luma Foundation, created in 2004 by Maja Hoffmann, was, like the Louis Vuitton Foundation, developed over an extended period of time, as is evident from the dozens of study models on the shelves of Frank Gehry's southern Californian studio. A stone's throw from the center of Arles and situated next to the Roman necropolis of the Alyscamps, Luma—named for the founder's children, Luca and Marina—redraws the historical silhouette of the city owing to its tower, which has come to dominate it. The final version of the project was the result of a great number of design studies, and its envelope was reduced to ten levels following pressure from local residents.

On the ground, the drum shape of the tower's lower levels is an imposing presence in the 7-ha.* Parc des Ateliers, where most of the hangars previously used for the maintenance and repair of the railroad have been transformed into exhibition spaces by the New York architect Annabelle Selldorf.

Here, the recurring duality of Gehry's buildings is inscribed vertically, the rectilinear prism of the circulation spaces serving as a buttress to the tower façades. The version ultimately chosen, following experiments with full-size simulations of some of its elements in the parking lot of the Playa Vista office, exemplifies the process that Gehry noted in the margins of one of his study sketches, and that he has never stopped searching for: "painting with the materials." In this case, the brushstrokes of the famous *Starry Night*, painted by Vincent van Gogh in Arles and a jewel in the collection of the Museum of Modern Art in New York, are transposed into metal. The volumes enclosing the studios, seminar rooms, and offices, which are clustered rather than assembled together to form the skin of the building, are finished off with 11,500 stainless-steel boxes. The cold and monochromatic quality of the material is transfigured by the light of France's Midi into multiple and changing hues, while crevasses cut zones of shadow into the volume of the tower. The fifty-three rectilinear glass cases that form the windows interrupt this sparkling whirlwind and give away the scale of the building by indicating the stacking of the floor levels within.

Inside the tower, the reticulated structure of reinforced concrete is left exposed instead of being hidden between the interior and exterior skins, as if in homage to the structural rationalism of Auguste Perret. The glazed drum sits between the undulating profile of the workshops, which are extended thanks to the opaque concrete volumes of the base that are devoted to exhibitions, and the shimmering tower above. It not only structures the transition between the program's different components, but also provides access to the foundation via a ribbon staircase outside. Set at the edge of the planted roadway that continues the boulevard des Lices and across from the new École Nationale Supérieure de la Photographie, the foundation effectively expands the perimeter of the city and forcefully expresses Arles's cultural and post-industrial vocation, which will no doubt also transform its population.

* 17-acre

View of the staircase and its reflection in the mirrored ceiling.

View of the tower from within the drum.

Appendixes

A Biographical Overview

1929 Frank Owen Goldberg is born in Toronto, Canada, to Isadore "Irving" Goldberg and his wife, Sadie "Thelma" Caplan, who were second-generation Jewish immigrants from the Russian Empire.

1934 Attends Alexander Muir Elementary School.

1935 Irving and Thelma give birth to a daughter, Doreen.

1937 The Goldbergs move to Timmins, Ontario, and Frank starts at Birch Street School, where he was first exposed to the game of hockey, which became a lasting passion.

1942 The Goldbergs return to Toronto, and Frank attends Bloor Collegiate for high school.

1946 Hears Alvar Aalto speak at a lecture series in Convocation Hall at the University of Toronto. This is considered his first serious introduction to architecture.

1947 Graduates from Bloor Collegiate and moves to Los Angeles, California, with his family. Starts taking free night classes at Los Angeles City College, but later that year enrolls at the University of Southern California (USC) in Los Angeles.

1948 Meets Anita Rae Snyder.

1949 Gains acceptance into the fine arts program at USC and specializes in design and ceramics. Takes courses with Glen Lukens, a prominent ceramicist who had recently worked with the modernist architect Raphael Soriano on the design of his house. Lukens introduces Frank to the architect and, upon seeing his student's enthusiasm for Soriano and his work, suggests that Frank give architecture a try.
Befriends USC architecture graduate student Arnold Schrier, who worked for the architect Frank Lloyd Wright. The two begin touring Los Angeles to look at modern structures, including those designed by Soriano and Lloyd Wright. Through Schrier, Frank meets the photographer Julius Shulman, who gives him access to see major modernist works in Los Angeles and introduces him to Richard Neutra and Rudolf Schindler.

1950 Becomes a US citizen and enrolls in the Air Force Reserve Officers' Training Corps.
Changes his major to architecture.

1951 Befriends fellow USC architecture classmate C. Gregory Walsh.
Does coursework with influential teachers who will come to inform his own practice. The architect Calvin Staub instills the importance of designing cities and neighborhoods in addition to buildings, and landscape architect Garrett Eckbo emphasizes the social responsibility of architecture. While at USC, Gehry also encounters instructors including Gregory Ain, Simon Eisner, Edgardo Contini, and William Pereira. During his time at USC, he also joins

Architecture Panel, a student-led group interested in the connection between architecture and social responsibility.

1952 Obtains a job at Victor Gruen Associates through his USC instructor Edgardo Contini, a partner at the firm. Marries Anita Snyder.

1953–54 With Rene Pesqueria and other USC colleagues, he forms the Collaborative Professional Planning Group in Los Angeles to plan a development in Baja California.

1954 Decides to changes his last name from Goldberg to Gehry.
Receives a Bachelor of Architecture degree at USC. Birth of Frank and Anita's first child, Leslie.

1955 Drafted into the U.S. Army, leaves for training at Fort Ord in northern California.

1956 Frank and Anita's second daughter, Brina, is born while the family is stationed in Atlanta, Georgia. Using funds provided by the 1944 G.I. Bill, he begins the urban planning program at the Harvard Graduate School of Design (GSD).

1957 Upon realizing he would be better suited to the architecture program, he begins to audit architecture courses at the GSD and becomes acquainted with Sigfried Giedion and Paul Rudolph. He also undertakes coursework with Otto Eckstein, John Gaus, Charles Haar, and Joseph Hudnut, among others. Takes a position at the Massachusetts architecture firm Perry, Shaw, Hepburn & Dean.
Recruited by Jack Bevash to join the Los Angeles firm Pereira & Luckman, which is headed by his former USC thesis advisor William Pereira.
Returns to work at Victor Gruen Associates.

1961 Moves to Paris with Anita and their two daughters and obtains a position at André Remondet's architecture practice. He also completes work for French planner Robert Auzelle. With the assistance of his former Harvard classmate Mark Biass, he visits historic buildings as well as modern examples in France, Switzerland, Germany, the Netherlands, Italy, and Spain. He is particularly inspired by Romanesque churches such as the abbey of Vézelay, and works by Le Corbusier and Gaudí will become important influences in his deviation from straight lines in his later designs.
The Gehrys return to Los Angeles in the summer. Does freelance work in Los Angeles for Carlos Diniz, a former Gruen employee and an artist who specializes in architectural renderings.
Opens the firm of Gehry & Walsh, Architects with Gregory Walsh, in a single room rented in a small house at 1448 5th Street in Santa Monica.

1964 Meets the Los Angeles artist Ed Moses during the construction of the Lou Danziger Studio.

This meeting is the start of a lifelong friendship, and Moses will also introduce him to the circle of artists who defined the Los Angeles group represented by the Ferus Gallery, including Ken Price, Billy Al Bengston, Ed Ruscha, and Chuck Arnoldi.

1966   Starts socializing with the psychotherapist Milton Wexler, an analyst for many Los Angeles creative figures, with whom he forms a friendship that would last for decades.
David O'Malley, a former colleague from Victor Gruen Associates, introduces him to the developer Jim Rouse of the Rouse Company. Upon securing work for Rouse's new development in Columbia, Maryland, he joins forces with O'Malley to form the twin-coastal firm of Gehry, Walsh & O'Malley, with his new partner based in Maryland.
Frank and Anita's marriage ends.

1967   Professionally parts ways with David O'Malley, and the firm is renamed Frank O. Gehry & Associates, Inc. It becomes large enough that he starts looking for an office manager. During this search he meets Berta Isabel Aguilera. She does not take the job, but the two begin dating.

1968   Participates with his sister Doreen in a pilot program called Artists-in-Schools, sponsored by the National Endowment for the Arts, and uses the principles of city planning to teach fifth graders.

1968–69   The office moves to 11632 San Vicente Boulevard in Brentwood.

1971   The office moves to 1524 Cloverfield Boulevard in Santa Monica.

1972   Travels to Finland with Berta and visits Alvar Aalto's architecture and furniture studio, although he does not get to meet Aalto.

1972–73   For the academic year, he acts as an assistant professor in the architecture department at his alma mater, USC.

1974   Elected to the College of Fellows at the American Institute of Architects.

1975   Receives a year-long teaching appointment at the recently formed Southern California Institute of Architecture.
Marries Berta Aguilera.

1976   Frank and Berta's first son, Alejandro, is born.

1977   Receives the Arnold W. Brunner Memorial Prize from the American Academy of Arts and Letters.
The Gehrys purchase a Dutch colonial house on 22nd Street in Santa Monica and transform it into their residence.

1979   Frank and Berta's second son, Sam, is born.
Establishes a short-lived joint firm with Boston architect Paul Krueger.

1987   Appointed a Fellow of the American Academy of Arts and Letters.

1988   The office moves back to 1520 Cloverfield Boulevard in Santa Monica.

1989   Receives the Pritzker Architecture Prize and is named trustee of the American Academy in Rome.

1991   The introduction of CATIA software reshapes the office's design process. Gehry is elected a Fellow of the American Academy of Arts and Sciences.

1992   Receives the Wolf Prize in Art (Architecture) from the Israeli Wolf Foundation and the Praemium Imperiale in Japan.

1994   Receives the Dorothy and Lillian Gish Prize for lifetime contribution to the arts and is elected an Academician of the National Academy of Design.

1998   Receives the Friedrich Kiesler Prize and the National Medal of Arts Award and is made an Honorary Academician at the Royal Academy of Arts.

1999   Receives the Gold Medal of the American Institute of Architects and the Medal of Merit from the Lotos Club.

2000   Awarded the Gold Medal by the Royal Institute of British Architects and the Lifetime Achievement Award by Americans for the Arts.

2002   Awarded the Gold Medal for Architecture by the American Academy of Arts and Letters.

2003   The office relocates to 12541 Beatrice Street in Playa Vista.
Made a Companion of the Order of Canada and elected a member of the European Academy of Sciences and Arts.

2006   Inducted to the California Hall of Fame by the governor of California.

2008   Receives the Golden Lion Lifetime Achievement award from the Venice Biennale.

2010   Receives the John Singleton Copley Award from the American Associates of the Royal Academy Trust and the Cooper Union for the Advancement of Science and Art Award.

2014   Made a Commander of the French Legion of Honor and receives the Prince of Asturias Award for the Arts.

2015   Receives the Getty Award for his contributions to and support for the arts.

2016   Receives the Leonore and Walter Annenberg Award for Diplomacy through the Arts and the Presidential Medal of Freedom from President Barack Obama.

2017   Awarded an honorary degree by the University of Oxford.

2018   Frank and Berta move to their new residence, Adelaide Drive in Santa Monica.

2021   Receives the National Sculpture Society's Henry Hering Art and Architecture Award for his distinguished use of sculpture at the Eisenhower Memorial.

Bibliography

Arnell, Peter, et al. *Frank Gehry: Buildings and Projects*. New York: Rizzoli, 1985.

Bechtler, Cristina, ed. *Frank O. Gehry, Kurt W. Forster*. Ostfildern: Cantz, 1999.

Bletter, Rosemarie Haag, ed. *The Architecture of Frank Gehry*. New York: Rizzoli, 1986.

Celant, Germano. *Frank O. Gehry: Since 1997*. Milan: Skira, 2009.

Cohen, Jean-Louis, ed. *Frank Gehry, Catalogue Raisonné of the Drawings: Volume One, 1954–1978*.
    Paris: Cahiers d'Art, 2020.

Da Costa Meyer, Esther. *Frank Gehry: On Line*. Princeton: Princeton University Art Museum, 2008.

Dal Co, Francesco, Kurt W. **Forster**, and Hadley S. **Arnold**. *Frank O. Gehry: The Complete Works*.
    New York: Monacelli Press, 1998.

Fernández-Galiano, Luis. *Frank Gehry 1985–1990*. Madrid: SGV, 1990.

Fernández-Galiano, Luis. *Gehry artista e icono*. Madrid: Arquitectura Viva, 2021.

Friedman, Mildred, ed. *Gehry Talks: Architecture + Process*. New York: Rizzoli, 1999.

Friedman, Mildred. *Frank Gehry: The Houses*. New York: Rizzoli, 2009.

Futagawa, Yukio. *Frank Gehry: Recent Project*. Tokyo: A.D.A. Edita, 2011.

Futagawa, Yukio, and Yoshio **Futagawa**. *Gehry x Futagawa*. Tokyo: A.D.A. Edita, 2015.

Gilbert-Rolfe, Jeremy. *Frank Gehry: The City and Music*. London and New York: Routledge, 2002.

Goldberger, Paul. *Building Art: The Life and Work of Frank Gehry*. New York: Alfred A. Knopf, 2015.

Isenberg, Barbara. *Conversations with Frank Gehry*. New York: Alfred A. Knopf, 2009.

Lemonier, Aurélien, and Frédéric **Migayrou**, eds. *Frank Gehry*. Munich: Prestel, 2015.

Levene, Richard C., and Cecilia F. **Márquez**. *Frank O. Gehry*. Madrid: El Croquis, 1990.

Levene, Richard C., and Cecilia F. **Márquez**. *Frank Gehry, 1991–1995*. Madrid: El Croquis, 1995.

Levene, Richard C., and Cecilia F. **Márquez**. *Frank Gehry, 1996–2003: From A to Z*. Madrid: El Croquis, 2003.

Levene, Richard C., and Cecilia F. **Márquez**. *Frank Gehry, 1987–2003*. Madrid: El Croquis, 2006.

Ragheb, J. Fiona., ed. *Frank Gehry, Architect*. New York: Guggenheim Museum Publications, 2001.

Rappolt, Mark, and Robert **Violette**, eds. *Gehry Draws*. Cambridge, MA: MIT Press, in association
    with Violette Editions, 2004.

Photographic Credits

Front cover: Stefano Politi Markovina/aw-images.com; p. 1: Tim Street-Porter/OTTO; p. 2: Thomas Mayer; p. 3: Matthew Carbone; p. 4: Andrew Worssam; p. 5: Atelier Vincent Hecht; p. 10: Amanda Demme; p. 20: Frank O. Gehry. Getty Research Institute, Los Angeles (2017.M.66), Frank Gehry Papers; pp. 22–23: All rights reserved; p. 24: Frank O. Gehry. Getty Research Institute, Los Angeles (2017.M.66), Frank Gehry Papers; p. 27 top: Frank O. Gehry. Getty Research Institute, Los Angeles (2017.M.66), Frank Gehry Papers; p. 27 bottom: All rights reserved; pp. 28, 31, and 33 top: Frank O. Gehry. Getty Research Institute, Los Angeles (2017.M.66), Frank Gehry Papers; p. 33 bottom: Michael Moran/OTTO; p. 34: Frank O. Gehry. Getty Research Institute, Los Angeles (2017.M.66), Frank Gehry Papers; p. 35: Michael Moran/OTTO; pp. 36–38: Frank O. Gehry. Getty Research Institute, Los Angeles (2017.M.66), Frank Gehry Papers; pp. 40–41: Marvin Rand; pp. 42–53: Frank O. Gehry. Getty Research Institute, Los Angeles (2017.M.66), Frank Gehry Papers; p. 55: All rights reserved; pp. 56–57: Jean-Louis Cohen; pp. 58–59: Patrick Corrigan; p. 60: Jean-Louis Cohen; pp. 62–63: Timothy Hursley; pp. 64–71: Tim Street-Porter/OTTO; pp. 72 and 73: All rights reserved; p. 74: Frank O. Gehry. Getty Research Institute, Los Angeles (2017.M.66), Frank Gehry Papers. Photo: Tim Street-Porter/OTTO; pp. 76–77: Michael Moran/OTTO; p. 78 top: Michael Moran/OTTO; p. 78 bottom: Frank O. Gehry. Getty Research Institute, Los Angeles (2017.M.66), Frank Gehry Papers; p. 81: Frank O. Gehry. Getty Research Institute, Los Angeles (2017.M.66), Frank Gehry Papers. Photo: Tim Street-Porter/OTTO; pp. 82–85: University of St. Thomas/Mike Ekern; p. 86: All rights reserved; p. 89: All rights reserved; pp. 90–91: Grant Mudford; p. 92: Michael Moran/OTTO; pp. 94–95: All rights reserved; p. 96: Timothy Hursley; p. 99: Timothy Hursley; p. 100: Michael Moran/OTTO; p. 101: Frank O. Gehry. Getty Research Institute, Los Angeles (2017.M.66), Frank Gehry Papers; p. 102: Jean-Louis Cohen; pp. 104–5: Michael Moran/OTTO; pp. 106 and 109: Timothy Hursley; p. 110: Jean-Louis Cohen; pp. 112–13: Tom Bonner; p. 114: Photo12/Alamy/Peter Cook; p. 117: Frank O. Gehry. Getty Research Institute, Los Angeles (2017.M.66), Frank Gehry Papers; pp. 118–19: Jean-Louis Cohen; p. 120: Grant Mudford; pp. 122–23: Jean-Louis Cohen; p. 124: Grant Mudford; p. 127: Grant Mudford; pp. 128–32: Frank O. Gehry. Getty Research Institute, Los Angeles (2017.M.66), Frank Gehry Papers; pp. 135–37: All rights reserved; p. 138: Grant Mudford; pp. 140–41: Tim Street-Porter/OTTO; pp. 142 and 145: Grant Mudford; pp. 146–47: Timothy Hursley; pp. 148–55: Vitra Design Museum. Photo: Norbert Miguletz; p. 156: Frank O. Gehry. Getty Research Institute, Los Angeles (2017.M.66), Frank Gehry Papers. Photo: Scott Francis/OTTO; pp. 158–59: Jean-Louis Cohen; p. 161: Collection Artedia/Bridgeman Images; p. 162: Emilio Colaiezzi/agefotostock; pp. 164–67: Tim Street-Porter/OTTO; p. 168: All rights reserved; p. 171: Courtesy of the Los Angeles Philharmonic Archives. Photo: Federico Zignani; pp. 172–73: All rights reserved; p. 174: Don Wong; p. 176: Jim Ericson; p. 178: Clément Guillaume/La Collection; p. 179: Weisman Art Museum/Rik Sferra; p. 181: Don Wong; p. 182: Photo12/Alamy/David Burton; pp. 184–85: FMGB Guggenheim Bilbao Museoa. Photo: Erika Barahone Ede; p. 186: Tim Graham/Getty Images; pp. 188–89: View Pictures/Universal Images Group via Getty Images/Richard Serra, Snake, 1994–97, Adagp, Paris, 2021; p. 191: Photo12/Alamy/John Gaffen; pp. 192–93: FMGB Guggenheim Bilbao Museoa. Photo: Erika Barahone Ede; p. 194: Rom/imageBROKER/Shutterstock; pp. 196–97: Photo12/Alamy/Igor Stevanovic; p. 198: All rights reserved; p. 201: Photo12/Alamy/EmmePi Stock Images; p. 202: akg-images/Bildarchiv Monheim; pp. 204–5: Photo12/Alamy/mauritius images GmbH; p. 206: Photo12/Alamy/Juergen Held/travelstock44; pp. 208–9: Thomas Mayer; p. 210: Roland Halbe; pp. 212–13: Thomas Mayer; pp. 214–15: Photo12/Alamy/Agencja Fotograficzna Caro; p. 217: Thomas Mayer; p. 218: Timothy Hursley; pp. 220–21: B.O'Kane/Alamy Stock Photo; pp. 222 and 225: Timothy Hursley; pp. 226–35: Peter Aaron/OTTO; pp. 236–40: Roland Halbe; p. 241: All rights reserved; pp. 243–45: Roland Halbe; p. 246: All rights reserved; pp. 248–50 and 253 top: Thomas Mayer; p. 253 bottom: Tourismus NRW e.V. (A1); pp. 254–55: Thomas Mayer; p. 256: Jon Arnold Images/hemis.fr; pp. 258–63: Patrick Pyszka/Chicago DCASE; pp. 264–71: Victoria Murillo/Istmophoto.com; p. 272: Art Gallery of Ontario; pp. 274–75: Photo12/Alamy/Radharc Images; pp. 276–79: Art Gallery of Ontario; p. 280: Thomas Mayer; pp. 282–83: Photo12/Alamy/Juan Carlos Munoz; pp. 284–89: Thomas Mayer; pp. 290–99: DBOX; p. 300: Emilio Collavino; pp. 302–3: Photography by Depuhl; p. 304: Claudia Uribe; p. 307: Iwan Baan; pp. 308–19: Iwan Baan; pp. 320–27: Matthew Carbone; pp. 328–30: Iwan Baan; p. 331: All rights reserved; pp. 332 and 335: Iwan Baan; pp. 336–37: Andrew Worssam; pp. 338–42: Courtesy of the Eisenhower Memorial Commission; commemorative design by Gehry Partners, LLP; tapestry by Tomas Osinski; sculpture by Sergey Eylanbekov; p. 345: Alan Karchmer/OTTO; pp. 346–47: Courtesy of the Eisenhower Memorial Commission; commemorative design by Gehry Partners, LLP; tapestry by Tomas Osinski; sculpture by Sergey Eylanbekov; pp. 348–59: Jason Schmidt; pp. 360–67: Roland Halbe; p. 368: Adrian Deweerdt/Fondation Luma; pp. 370–71: Iwan Baan; pp. 372–75: Adrian Deweerdt/Fondation Luma; pp. 377 and 378: Iwan Baan; back cover: Claudia Uribe.

Acknowledgments

The author expresses his sincere gratitude to all those who allowed this book to come to fruition. First and foremost, Frank and Berta Gehry, Meaghan Lloyd, Joyce Shin, and Megan Meulemans. The team at the Getty Research Institute, which holds the archives of the early period of Gehry's work, under the direction of Maristella Casciato, allowed the author to consult documents that were crucial to the comprehension of the architect's designs. The author wishes to thank all the former clients and current occupants, who not only gave him access to the buildings, but also shared their reminiscences of their genesis and use. He is indebted to the former members of the office in Santa Monica, Venice, and Playa Vista, the memories of whom remain irreplaceable.

Cahiers d'Art and Staffan Ahrenberg extend their warmest thanks to Frank Gehry and Meaghan Lloyd for their invaluable assistance; Jean-Louis Cohen for the precision and clarity of his text; Rik Bas Backer and José Albergaria at the studio Change is Good for the elegance and dynamism of their graphic design; and Julie Rouart and the team at Flammarion for their expertise.

The Author

Jean-Louis Cohen is an acclaimed historian, critic, and curator of architecture and urban design. He holds the Sheldon H. Solow Chair at New York University's Institute of Fine Arts and has curated numerous exhibitions at the Museum of Modern Art, the Canadian Center for Architecture, the Centre Georges Pompidou, the Cité de l'Architecture et du Patrimoine, and MAXXI. He is the author of more than forty books, and his first volume of the catalogue raisonné of Frank Gehry's drawings was published by Cahiers d'Art in 2020.

21 22 23 3 2 1
Legal Deposit: 11/2021

Cahiers d'Art, Paris
Publisher
Staffan Ahrenberg
Editorial Director
Séverine Schulte

Flammarion, Paris
French Edition
Editorial Director
Julie Rouart
Editor
Marion Doublet, assisted by Dorine Morgado and Marie-Lou Étienne
Editorial Administration Manager
Delphine Montagne
Picture Research
Marie Audet and Sandrine Fournié

English Edition
Editorial Director
Kate Mascaro
Editor
Helen Adedotun
Copyediting
Sam Wythe
Proofreading
Sarah Kane

Design and Typesetting
Change is Good, Paris
assisted by Antoine Mozziconacci

Production
Corinne Trovarelli
Color Separation
Fotimprim, Paris
Printed in Spain by Indice

Simultaneously published in French as
Frank Gehry: Les Chefs-d'œuvre
© Flammarion, S.A., Paris, 2021
English-language edition
© Flammarion, S.A., Paris, 2021
87, quai Panhard et Levassor, 75647 Paris Cedex 13
editions.flammarion.com
ISBN Flammarion: 978-2-08-024850-3
© Cahiers d'Art, Paris, 2021
14, rue du Dragon, 75006 Paris
cahiersdart.com
ISBN Cahiers d'Art: 9782851173232
© Frank Gehry for his works